Competition and Free Trade

The concepts of competition and free trade are absolutely central for the understanding of human societies but are also often subject to fear and criticism. It is not possible to understand what competition really is without referring to the concept of freedom; free trade must be understood, also, as the way to expand the scope of competition.

This book analyzes the two concepts as closely interlinked by approaching them in two parts. The first, 'Competition', introduces the reader to the traditional competition model, and explores the dynamics and range of the term in an authoritative way. The second part, 'Free Trade', examines the different types of trade, and analyzes them in a wealth of contexts, from customs duties to import quotas. With discussions of protectionist arguments, politics, liberalization, and history, the author presents an overview of how competition and free trade operate in the real world.

This book dispels the fears and misunderstandings that have developed around these central pillars of the modern economy. It is essential reading for those studying international economics, international trade, political economy, or corporate finance.

Pascal Salin is Honorary Professor of Economics at Université Paris – Dauphine, France.

Routledge Foundations of the Market Economy

Edited by Mario J. Rizzo, New York University, and Lawrence H. White, George Mason University

For a full list of titles in this series, please visit www.routledge.com/series/SE0104

A central theme in this series is the importance of understanding and assessing the market economy from a perspective broader than the static economics of perfect competition and Pareto optimality. Such a perspective sees markets as causal processes generated by the preferences, expectations, and beliefs of economic agents. The creative acts of entrepreneurship that uncover new information about preferences, prices, and technology are central to these processes with respect to their ability to promote the discovery and use of knowledge in society.

The market economy consists of a set of institutions that facilitate voluntary cooperation and exchange among individuals. These institutions include the legal and ethical framework as well as more narrowly 'economic' patterns of social interaction. Thus the law, legal institutions, and cultural and ethical norms, as well as ordinary business practices and monetary phenomena, fall within the analytical domain of the economist.

Competition and Free Trade

Pascal Salin

Routledge
Taylor & Francis Group

LONDON AND NEW YORK

First published 2018 by Routledge

2 Park Square, Milton Park, Abingdon, Oxfordshire OX14 4RN
52 Vanderbilt Avenue, New York, NY 10017

Routledge is an imprint of the Taylor & Francis Group, an informa business

First issued in paperback 2019

British Library Cataloguing-in-Publication Data
A catalogue record for this book is available from the British Library

Library of Congress Cataloging-in-Publication Data
Names: Salin, Pascal, author.
Title: Competition and free trade / Pascal Salin.
Description: New York : Routledge, 2018. | Includes bibliographical
    references and index.
Identifiers: LCCN 2017016233 | ISBN 9781138103436 (hardback) |
    ISBN 9781315102726 (ebook)
Subjects: LCSH: Competition. | Free trade. | Protectionism.
Classification: LCC HF1414 .S25 2018 | DDC 338.5/22—dc23
LC record available at https://lccn.loc.gov/2017016233

ISBN: 978-1-138-10343-6 (hbk)
ISBN: 978-0-367-88891-6 (pbk)

Typeset in Times New Roman
by Apex CoVantage, LLC

For Balthazar,
my grandson,
to whom I wish a happy life in freedom.

Contents

Foreword

Why do we analyze competition and freedom of trade in the same book? First, because both these concepts are absolutely central for the understanding of human societies, and second, these two concepts are closely interlinked. In fact, as we will see, it is not possible to understand what competition really is without referring to the concept of freedom. And free trade must precisely be analyzed as the way to expand the scope of competition. Even though these two concepts are studied in two different parts of this book, there is a real continuity in the analysis of these phenomena and neither of these parts is understandable without referring to the other one.

Competition, as well as freedom of trade, are often mentioned, but they are also often subject to fears and criticisms that this book is trying to dispel. This is why, beyond the single thought on these phenomena, we hope that this book will provide answers to important concerns of real life.

Part I
Competition

Introduction

The concept of competition is frequently used in daily life. One speaks of competing sportsmen as well as pupils in a school, or firms that are competing in a market, or politicians who compete for a position in an election. The analysis of competition also plays a central role in economic theory. In fact the working of markets is not the same whether there is competition or not. But still one needs to know how it is defined. There is from this point of view a traditional theory of competition, the so-called theory of pure and perfect competition, which one can also call the theory of atomistic competition (because producers are analyzed as simple 'atoms' of something much broader than them). This same theory analyzes a monopoly or a cartel by reference to the situation assumed to be optimal, namely pure and perfect competition. This traditional theory is dominant in textbooks and in a great part of economic literature. It also inspires what is called, for instance, competition policy (or antitrust policy). It is questionable, however, as we show in the present book. Oddly enough, it is rather the concept of competition used in everyday life that gives a correct vision of what it is, whereas the traditional theory is based on a purely formal approach that is not really able to explain reality. Another approach to competition must therefore be developed in economic theory: that of free competition, i.e. the one that corresponds to the possibility to freely enter into a market. The result is a totally different appreciation of monopolies or cartels, which may, depending on their specific characteristics, have a harmful role or, on the contrary, be useful in meeting some specific needs of markets and in being key factors of innovation and economic progress.

1 The traditional competition model

Given the importance of the traditional theory of competition as a central model of economic theory and as a reference for policy decisions, it is necessary to identify which are the critical assumptions and the essential implications of this theory. It goes further than the simple analysis of a situation of competition: it turns into a normative theory by demonstrating that competition leads to an economic optimum.

The characteristics of 'atomistic' competition

In an exchange economy, each good corresponds to a market: an abstract place in which the supply and the demand for a good are confronting. From the confrontation of supply and demand a price is determined, which one calls an 'equilibrium price' as far as it corresponds to the wishes of buyers and sellers of this good.

If there is competition on a market, the price of the corresponding good is exactly the same all over its market: the price of one pound of wheat is the same on the entire wheat market. This is the 'law of one price', which results from simple assumptions concerning the behaviour of economic agents. It is just assumed that, generally speaking, individuals, be they suppliers or buyers, are able to compare prices. A buyer will look for the lowest possible price, a supplier will wish to obtain the highest possible price. If a producer offers a good at a higher price than the one proposed by all other suppliers, he will obviously not sell his commodity and, if he wants to stay on the market, he must align his prices on those of his competitors. Symmetrically, if his price is lower than the one offered by his competitors, he will be encouraged to increase it (and possibly to increase the amount of supplied goods) in order to increase his profits. Thus, as soon as one has done the simple assumption according to which individuals who act on a market are able to compare prices and to assess their own interests, it follows that there is a single price for one given good.

The implementation of a single price depends on the existence of several producers placed in a situation of competition, which means that their products are likely to be the subject of comparisons and that these products are perceived by buyers as exactly identical one to each other. But to what extent can we say that there is competition? This is the problem we have to solve.

There is from this point of view what can be called a *traditional theory of competition* which one finds, for instance, with a number of variants, in virtually all the textbooks of microeconomics. But let us first accept a convention of language. We will see later that this traditional definition, still widely used, is extremely questionable. We must therefore distinguish between the traditional concept of competition and the concept that we will suggest later, which we will call 'free competition'. Now, the traditional approach is characterised by the fact that it implies the existence of a large number of producers and buyers, so that each of them can be considered as an 'atom' of this great set of individuals who are acting in markets. We will therefore use the term *atomistic competition* to refer to the traditional concept of competition.[1]

To clarify the traditional concept of competition let us take, for instance, the definition given by George Stigler[2]: 'A competitive market can be defined easily only as a perfect market; it is a market on which the price will be influenced neither by the purchases nor by the sales of a single person. In other words, with regard of any buyer, the elasticity of supply is infinite; with regard to any seller, the elasticity of demand is infinite.'

Let us just recall that the price elasticity is defined as the ratio of the variation in quantity (demanded or supplied) in comparison to the variation of price.[3] Thus saying that the elasticity of supply is infinite is saying that no price change is possible (an infinitesimal variation in the price would result in an infinite variation of available quantities). In Stigler's definition, then, there is competition whenever no producer can be considered as different from others: Competition is thus of the atomistic kind.

If one adopts this approach to competition, a market can be competitive only so far as it is 'perfect'. Let us imagine an area in which there are many bakers, each producing only one perfectly well-defined good, namely a one-pound loaf that has exactly the same characteristics (say, its taste, its appearance, and the length of its preserving period). One can therefore consider that these different loaves are perfectly substitutable one to the other from the point of view of their *physical characteristics* or even from a subjective point of view, namely their ability to meet the needs of potential consumers of bread. But let us imagine that it is very difficult to move inside this region and that the inhabitants live in communities that are very isolated from each other. Information about the price of bread will be extremely limited, without even mentioning the possibility of carrying a loaf from one place to another. From an *economic point of view*, one can therefore consider that the different loaves are not perfectly substitutable: The bread produced in A is specific, and the baker who produces it may ask a price different from the one that is demanded by the baker B. The 'atomistic' definition of competition leads therefore to considering that there is no competition, as far as there is a differentiation of goods. We will have the opportunity later on to revisit the relationship that may exist between differentiation of goods and competition. But we will retain, in any case, this idea that it is not only the physical characteristics of the goods which matter, but rather their subjective and economic characteristics. Two goods are different from an economic point of view, if they are perceived as different by one or more individuals, taking into account the uses they intend to give to these goods.

Atomistic competition cannot therefore be conceived other than concerning a 'perfect market': a market where information is perfect, ensuring a single price for each of the goods that are perfectly substitutable. For this traditional theory of competition, any competitive market is necessarily perfect, but any perfect market is not competitive. For a market to be competitive – that it is, according to the usual terminology, in a situation of 'pure and perfect competition' – some other specific features must be added.

The traditional theory naturally cares about the conditions that are necessary for competition to exist, those that allow the existence of a single price on the market and which prevent a producer from proposing a price different from that of 'competitors' for the same good. The list of these conditions differs slightly according to different authors, but there are in general the following elements[4]:

- Perfect information, of course
- The existence of a large number of buyers and sellers, each having a small economic dimension in relation to others
- An homogeneous product
- A divisible product

This list of conditions – common to most authors – seems obvious if one relates it to the essential concern of the traditional theory. In fact, competition is defined by its 'atomistic' nature: Each seller or each buyer is of negligible importance in relation to the whole market of a given good. The existence of a large number of buyers and sellers plays a particularly important role in the traditional theory of competition. This implies that each market participant is interchangeable and that none has sufficient weight for any individual decision to have an influence on the market. If a seller or a buyer withdraws from the market for a good, the price of this good is absolutely not modified. If each produced good could be differentiated from others, it would not be true that each seller or buyer is of negligible importance compared to the whole market for a good. Therefore, for pure and perfect competition to prevail, it is necessary not only that there be a large number of sellers and buyers, but also that the goods that they exchange be undifferentiated (which excludes the case of an indivisible good with a great economic size) and that the information about them be perfect. The list of conditions that must be met so that there is atomistic competition is therefore nothing more than a consequence of this idea that no consumer and no producer can affect the market price of a good. If the goods are not perfectly identical, the behaviour of a producer or a buyer of a good slightly different from others will influence the price of this specific good. Consider, for instance, the case of one pound of pleasantly packed arabica coffee. There may be a large number of buyers, but only one producer, and he thus enjoys a certain margin of freedom to determine his prices. In other words one should perhaps not mention in this case the market for coffee in general, but the 'market for a nicely packed arabica coffee'. The fact remains, however, that there is a very strong substitutability between these neighbouring products, so that the price of a good slightly different from the others cannot evolve in a perfectly independent way. If it increased too much, buyers would leave it to buy a close substitute. Whatever it is, the divisible character of a good makes more likely the existence of a large number of producers and buyers: atomistic competition is more likely to exist in the market for wheat than in the market for nuclear power plants.

The traditional theory implies that there is no pure and perfect competition, for instance, in markets such as the market for nuclear power plants or the market for big planes. But it has an implication which is more subtle and probably more threatening for the theory in question, as we will see: the definition of the characteristics of a good is necessarily arbitrary, all the more so since one should distinguish its purely physical characteristics and its subjectively perceived characteristics. Thus, if the inhabitants of an area are sensitive to the personality of the bakers who sell bread to them, loaves with identical physical characteristics but sold by different bakers will be considered by them as different. Should we then mention a bread market – in which there would be a large number of sellers – or a bread market A, a bread market B, and so on? The precise delimitation of an economic good, and therefore of the limits of what constitutes a 'market', by an outside observer being necessarily arbitrary, it becomes also arbitrary to decide whether there is a large number of sellers. We will come back later to this problem.

Another condition of competition is often but not always stated: the freedom of entry into a market. For the advocates of the theory of pure and perfect competition – unlike what we shall see later – this condition is important only insofar as it can be connected to what is almost the only criterion of competition: the existence of many producers and sellers. One can indeed consider that this criterion is more likely to be satisfied whenever it is possible to enter freely into a market. And it is precisely because the freedom of entry into a market is only a derived condition (considered traditionally) that it is sometimes omitted from the list of the conditions that are necessary for competition to exist.

Generally speaking, we can say that the traditional theory of competition is based on a single criterion: the great number of buyers and sellers for one given good. But for each author the list of conditions that must be met for competition to exist is shorter or longer, more or less comparable to the lists of other authors. One may consider the nature of the goods (homogeneity, indivisibility) as well as the behaviour of participants in the market (freedom of entry) or the characteristics of the processes (quality of information). And if the criterion of the great number of participants in the market is thus put forward, it is because it admits the particular case of the general theory of prices – an infinite elasticity of the supply curve, or of the demand curve, that an individual must face. For the supplier as well as for the buyer, the price is given by 'the market' and no one is able to influence it.

The implications of the traditional theory

One can draw important consequences from the traditional theory of competition; some of these inspire many laws and regulations. First we will see how the relationship between the working of the market and an individual producer is analyzed within this theory, and second, how this theory becomes normative.

Competition and market equilibrium

To understand the scope of the traditional theory of competition, it is convenient to use the usual instruments of microeconomic analysis. Let us imagine, then, a world where there are, for the sake of simplicity, two goods, wheat and tomatoes, but where there are many producers of both these goods. Let us also assume for the time being that there is no money, so that we are in a barter economy. It is usual in microeconomic theory to speak of the 'wheat market' and of the 'price of wheat', or, of course, to speak of the 'tomato market' and of the 'price of tomatoes'. In fact, in a market, one always trades a good against another. In other words, under the simplified assumption we have chosen, the wheat market is actually the set of all transactions by which some people supply wheat and demand tomatoes (they are called 'wheat suppliers'), while others demand wheat and supply tomatoes (they are called 'wheat demanders'). The wheat market is therefore actually a market of 'wheat against tomatoes'. Similarly, what is called the 'price' of one pound of wheat represents the quantity of tomatoes that can be obtained on the market in exchange for one pound of wheat, tomatoes being thus used as a standard of value: one says, for instance, that 1 pound of wheat 'costs' 2 pounds of tomatoes; that is, it is traded against 2 pounds of tomatoes.[5]

Let us thus represent this 'wheat market'. In Figure 1.1 we have depicted the quantity of wheat demanded or supplied – on the abscissa axis – in relation to the price of wheat (expressed in terms of pounds of tomatoes or in terms of currency units). The general forms of the supply and demand curves correspond

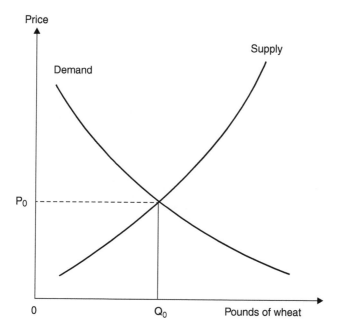

Figure 1.1

to simple assumptions concerning the rational nature of human behaviour. All human activity is indeed the outcome of arbitrations between potential uses of available resources, whether they are time, land, capital, or other resources. Thus, a producer of wheat will be prepared to give his first pound of wheat against a 'small' amount of tomatoes. In fact, to perform this production, he would have, for instance, to sacrifice one hour of leisure and, as he is not very busy for the time being, this sacrifice will easily be accepted. But the more he will increase his scale of production, the more the opportunity cost of wheat production will be perceived as high for him in terms of leisure time (or other resources). Moreover, he will be less and less eager to buy tomatoes.

It is therefore logical that the supply curve for a good (in relation to another) be increasing relative to its price. Similarly it is logical that the demand curve be decreasing: one is all the more encouraged to buy a good when it is cheaper, which means that one has to deliver a smaller quantity of another good. In Figure 1.1, P_0 and Q_0 represent respectively the equilibrium price and the equilibrium quantity on the market: that is, the values of these variables that satisfy both suppliers and demanders. This price and this quantity are determined by the countless wishes and actions of a very large number of suppliers and demanders, in accordance with the assumption of the traditional theory of competition.

In Figure 1.2, one can see represented the characteristics of a producer of wheat (any one among the countless producers who exist in the traditional model of competition). For the time being we consider a short-run situation: one in which a firm cannot change its production process or the amount of production factors

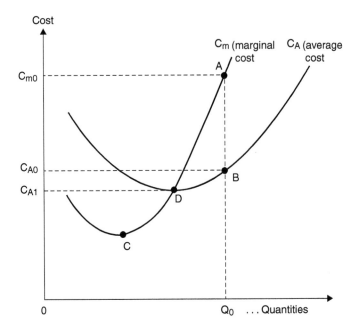

Figure 1.2

at its disposal. It is traditional to express the characteristics and the workings of a firm under the form of an average cost curve and a marginal cost curve.[6] The quantities that are produced are represented on the x-axis and the cost of production is shown on the y-axis. The average cost curve (C_A) shows the cost of production per unit of product in relation to the amount produced. Obviously, it is obtained by dividing the total cost of production of the firm (C_T) by the number of units produced. The marginal cost curve (C_m) indicates the additional cost that the firm must bear to produce one additional unit. Let us assume that at some given point in time the firm produces a quantity Q_0. The average cost for this level of production is equal to C_{A0} (ordinate of point B). To produce an additional unit the firm should accept an increase in costs equal to C_{m0} (ordinate of point A).

It is not necessary to specify in detail the reasons that explain the general form of these two curves,[7] but this rationale can be summarised as follows. The evolution of costs in relation to the scale of production results from the combination of two phenomena that play in opposite directions. Total production costs (C_T) can be broken down into two parts, fixed costs (C_{FT}) and variable costs (C_{VT}). Fixed costs are independent of the scale of production, so that the average and marginal fixed costs decrease when the scale of production is increasing. They are spread over a greater number of produced units. Variable costs change in reverse, first because one begins by using the more efficient production processes at a small scale of production, then one has to use more and more expensive means to produce more (overtime work hours, more obsolete machines, and so on). But this evolution depends also on a reason we have already encountered: that the opportunity cost increases with the scale of production. The greater the quantity produced, the more costly is the sacrifice in renouncing the use of available resources to produce other goods and services. Thus, when starting from a position where the production is zero (point O) and one gradually increases this production, the decrease in fixed costs per unit is predominant; then the increase in unit variable costs has more and more influence, so that the average and marginal cost curves increase. Moreover, let us recall that the relative positions of the curves C_A and C_m correspond to what is plotted in Figure 1.2: The marginal cost curve C_m reaches a minimum (point C) before the average cost curve C_A (its minimum is at point D, at which the curve C_m is crossing the curve C_A).[8]

Taking these instruments into account, what can we understand concerning the consequences for the behaviour of the entrepreneur?

There is a first requirement: that the production be profitable. Therefore the firm compares the market price of its product and its unit production costs. If the market price of one unit is just equal to C_{A1}, the profit per unit – the difference between the sale price and the average cost of production – is nil. Of course, if the market price was less than C_{A1}, the firm would incur losses and it would finally fail – disappear from the market. We thus arrive at a first conclusion: For the firm to be induced to produce, its average production cost must not be higher than the sale price, which is obvious.

But what is the precise level of production which is optimal? In Figure 1.3, we put together Figure 1.1 (inverted on the left quadrant) and Figure 1.2.[9] Since it is assumed that a situation of 'pure and perfect competition' prevails, the dimension

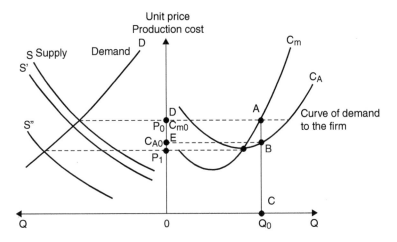

Figure 1.3

of the individual firm represented on the right of the figure is so small in relation to the overall set of producers of the same product that it has no discernible
influence on the supply curve represented on the left of Figure 1.3. It remains in
the same position regardless of the quantity produced by the firm. For this firm,
therefore, the price is 'given' by the market, it is equal in the present case to P_0. It
can be said that the straight line DA represents the demand curve, which the firm
specifically faces. It is perfectly inelastic (price change is impossible), whereas
the demand curve that concerns the whole market (left quadrant) is elastic.[10]

It is thus in the firm's interest to produce the quantity Q_0 because it is this
level of production that provides the maximum profit. In fact, if it produced one
additional unit, the marginal cost of this unit would be greater than P_0, which is
the amount one would get from its sale. In reverse, if the firm was producing one
less unit, the marginal cost would be lower than the sale price, there would be an
untapped profit opportunity. In Figure 1.3 total costs are represented by the area of
the rectangle BCOE (average cost multiplied by the quantity produced), total revenues by ACOD (sale price, P_0, multiplied by the quantity sold) and the total profit
of the firm is therefore represented by the area of the rectangle ABED, that is, the
difference between total revenues and total costs. Given the state of the market,
the area of this rectangle is at maximum when the firm equates the marginal cost
with the market price.

But is this the end of the story? Certainly not. We have just seen, in fact, that,
given the state of the market, there was a possibility of profit – with a maximum
value equal to ABED – for the firm studied. Then it is likely that other firms
will be tempted to enter into the market for this good. In accordance with the
assumptions of the so-called pure and perfect competition, we assumed a world
of perfect information, which implies in particular that the knowledges concerning the production processes flow instantly and for free, in such a way that every
entrepreneur can use the best techniques known to produce the studied good. It
is normal, under such a set of assumptions, to assume that all firms – existing or

potential – have exactly the same average and marginal cost curves.[11] The right quadrant of Figure 1.3 represents what might be called the 'representative firm': Exactly the same figure can be made for each enterprise and the aggregation of all these figures gives the overall supply curve located in the left quadrant.

But let us imagine that the representative firm is located in the position shown in Figure 1.3 (with a unit profit equal to AB) and that new firms arrive on this market, attracted by the rate of profit they can make. The quantity of the good supplied will increase, resulting in a shift toward the left of the aggregate supply curve (shift from S to S' on the left quadrant). The price of the market, determined by the intersection between the aggregate demand curve (which does not move) and the aggregate supply curve, will therefore decrease as fast as new firms enter into the market for this good. The process will stop when the number of (identical) firms will be such that the total supply will be S'. The market price will be equal to P_1, which means that the selling price of the studied good will be just equal to the average cost of production of all firms. As we have seen, the profit is then zero. If new firms entered into the market, the profit would become negative and some firms would therefore go bankrupt. But the profit having become nil, no more firm is induced to enter into this market.

The assumption of free entry on the market, which we have met previously, therefore leads to this conclusion: In the 'pure and perfect competition' case, the profit of entrepreneurs becomes zero. Such a result is obtained more or less rapidly, according to the rhythm of entry of firms on the market. This situation is described by the traditional theory as a situation of stable equilibrium.

Of course, this conclusion is the outcome of a crucial assumption, namely that all firms are absolutely identical. If one drops this assumption, there is a situation similar to that of Figure 1.4 (where we have merely represented the position of

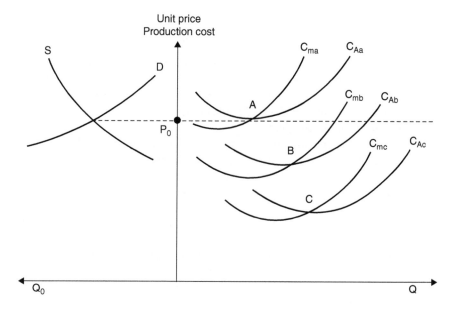

Figure 1.4

only three firms, A, B, and C). The less efficient firm, A, gets no profit since its average cost is equal to the market price, P_0. But the firms B and C get a profit. According to the traditional theory, this situation is obviously not stable. In this world of supposed perfection, the more efficient production techniques, those of B and, above all, C, are freely available. Therefore firm A will perhaps adopt these techniques or others will do it. In the latter case, the increase of production that thus occurs and the corresponding decrease in the market price put firm A in a situation of bankruptcy. It will have to get out of the market to leave room for the newly arrived firms. Whatever is the process, therefore, all firms will converge toward a single model and, in this world where everything is undifferentiated, the profit will become zero. Such is the consistency of the traditional theory. Everything is 'perfect', there is no differentiation, either between goods or between firms.

But if this undifferentiation between firms does not exist, it would be because perfect competition between firms does not exist, according to the traditional theory of competition. It may happen, in particular, that there are production factors so specific that the entry of new 'competing' firms is impossible. Thus there is a very limited area to produce wine with the name 'Vosne-Romanée-Conti', so that free entry on the market for this specific wine cannot exist. In such a case, the traditional theory would say that the owner of a land of this kind benefits from a 'rent'. The existence of a rent would thus mean that competition does not prevail.

The traditional theory goes further, however: it considers that pure and perfect competition represents 'the best of worlds'. But very precise conditions have to be met for competition to exist. If these conditions are not met, then one is not in the best of all worlds. Solutions must be found to try to move closer to such a situation. It is this normative character of the traditional theory which we are now examining.

The normative theory of competition: the economic optimum

The traditional theory of competition makes a further step when it shifts from the positive analysis that we just considered to a normative theory of the economy. The shift from a theory of economic equilibrium to a theory of economic optimum has been the subject of sophisticated mathematical analyses, but we will be content here with a simplified approach.

The wishes of the members of a society are a priori irreconcilable. The one who supplies a good would like to get as high a price as possible, while the demander would like a price as low as possible. Agreements are possible between demanders and suppliers; this is reflected by the existence of an equilibrium point on the graph of supply and demand. At this point everyone gets the greatest possible satisfaction, taking into account the environment in which he or she is located, which includes in particular the existence of partners in exchange whose needs and claims are initially divergent. It can be said that each individual is thus in an optimal position, otherwise she or he would not do what she or he is doing. Thus, for a certain price P_0 prevailing on the market for a good, the individual decides to supply or to purchase a certain quantity of this good in exchange for a certain amount of another good, to sacrifice leisure or to get some more of it, to borrow or to loan, and so on.

Each individual is able to choose among different options available; one can claim 'I prefer x to y'. But one cannot – and in fact one does not try to – quantify the satisfaction that one gets from each possible action. This quantification is a fortiori even more inconceivable for an outside observer. This means that it is impossible to define a 'social optimum' that would somehow be the sum of all the individual optima.[12] Therefore, whenever one says that a situation of economic optimum has been reached, this does not mean that the members of the considered society are in the best possible situations, since an absolute judgment of this kind can have no legitimacy.

It is in a more restricted sense that one can speak of an optimum (since the concept of optimum can actually have no meaning except from the point of view of an individual). One will thus say that an optimum is reached if, for a certain state of a society[13] – the capacities, the resources, the tastes of its members – equilibrium is achieved on all markets. In this case, in fact, one cannot increase the well-being of an individual without diminishing the well-being of another individual. If we consider the traditional graph of supply and demand (Figure 1.1), and if we want, for instance, to increase the well-being of a demander, it is necessary to decrease the price of what he or she is demanding. But this reduction in price obviously decreases the satisfaction of at least one supplier. There is no way to say that the increase of satisfaction of the first individual has 'offset' – or even done more that 'offset' – the decrease of satisfaction of the latter, since it is impossible to compare satisfactions. This equivalence between the achievement of equilibrium on all markets and a certain social optimum does exist, according to the traditional theory, insofar as there is pure and perfect competition in all these markets. If the conditions of pure and perfect competition are not met in some markets, there is no guarantee that the price system spontaneously leads to an optimum, even in the relative meaning of the optimum that has been stated above.[14] The traditional theory therefore leads to the conclusion that a social optimum is reached (for a given initial state of the society and of resources), when each person can act freely and can express his wishes to supply or to demand on free markets, provided that there is pure and perfect competition. One could interpret this theory as a justification for a market economy, and some people even consider that it is a demonstration of the superiority of capitalism.[15]

But it can also be used to reach almost opposite conclusions. In fact, as we have just recalled, one demonstrates that, according to the traditional theory, the free working of markets leads to an optimum, provided that competition is pure and perfect. However, since it is exceptional that all the conditions of pure and perfect competition be fulfilled in the real working of markets, it can be concluded that one can never reach a social optimum by relying on the free functioning of markets. When reality has the bad taste to not comply with the theoretical model, rather than changing the theoretical model one will transform the reality so that it approximates the theoretical model, thus forcing markets to behave 'as if' pure and perfect competition prevailed. But, in so doing, one collides with a major obstacle. In fact, one can always express the view that the actual working of any market does not exactly match what would be required by the theoretical model. But from which limit can one assume that the requirements can be regarded as fulfilled or not? How many firms, for instance, ought to be in a market for pure and perfect competition to exist? Every economist, every observer, every politician can give his own assessment without any possible way to decide between them. Oddly enough, the traditional theory of competition, the sophistication of which can give the feeling that it is a perfectly scientific approach,[16] leads to a situation in which the personal opinions of everyone are substituted to a scientific analysis.

The traditional theory of competition has thus surreptitiously transformed a positive theory of markets into a normative theory. General economic equilibrium and optimum, as they can be defined from the assumptions of the model, have become the standard against which the working of an economy should be judged. Any deviation from the standard would therefore require corrections that might be made by an affirmative action interfering with the free functioning of markets. As we have seen, for the traditional theory, the competitive character of a market is based essentially on the more or less large number of participants in this market (producers and consumers). All the conditions that one can imagine for competition to be 'pure and perfect' are actually conditions to ensure that there is a large number of participants. Thus, freedom of entry into a market – to which we give a great importance subsequently – is useful in the traditional theory only insofar as it allows the maintenance of a large number of producers. But why should we worry about the number of producers or consumers? Because, when producers are numerous, none of them can individually have any influence on the market.

One can therefore say that what is interesting from the point of view of the traditional theory is that no producer can have a particular power compared to other producers or consumers. Similarly, because consumers are very numerous, none of them can have a particular power. But what happens, according to the traditional theory, if there are asymmetries of power? This is what we will now consider.

Notes

1 In traditional theory it is rather called the theory of 'pure and perfect competition'. This expression, which we will find below, has an excessively normative tone, so that we prefer to use the expression 'atomistic competition'.
2 Stigler (1966). One would find similar definitions in a very large number of books.
3 More precisely, the price elasticity is defined as the relative variation of the quantity demanded or supplied in relation to the price variation:
4 Here we refer again to George Stigler (1966).
5 In the monetary economies that we know, it is customary to trade a good against money, so that the supply of wheat is a supply of wheat against a demand for money. In the same way, what is commonly referred to as 'the price of wheat' is the price of wheat in terms of money. More information can be found on the exact meaning of the supply and demand curves in our book *The International Monetary System and the Theory of Monetary Systems* (Salin 2016).
6 We use this same presentation on several occasions, to describe the traditional theory of competition as well as to criticise it. In other words, these instruments should not be considered as specific to a particular theory; they have a broader scope.

7 One may refer to any textbook of microeconomics for this.

8 In fact, the cost function being C(q), where C is the cost and q the quantity produced, the average cost is defined by $C_A(q) = C(q)/q$ and the marginal cost, C_m, by the derivative C'(q). At the minimum of the average cost curve, the derivative of the average cost over the quantity is zero, which implies that $dC_A(q)/dq = (C'(q).q - C(q))/q2 = 0$ and thus $C'(q) = C(q)/q = C_A(q)$, i.e. the marginal cost and the average cost are equal when the average cost is minimum.

9 Of course, the scale of the axis of quantities is not the same on the left quadrant and on the right quadrant: The quantities produced by the firm represented on the right are extremely small compared to the quantities traded on the market (left quadrant).

10 In a symmetric way, from the point of view of a specific demander the supply curve is infinitely elastic: He can buy a very great quantity of a good without any price change.

11 This assumes, of course, that they pay the different factors of production – work, capital, land – at identical rates. But it is precisely the case if the markets for the factors of production are also 'pure and perfect': The market requires, for instance, an identical hourly wage for the workers with a certain qualification, regardless of the precise job worked.

12 This has been stressed, in particular, by the theorists of "welfare economics". But strangely, one often reasons as if this impossibility did not exist.

13 It is frequently said that this proposal is valid for a certain initial "allocation" of resources. This term is ambiguous because it suggests that the resources owned by each individual results from a distribution made by some central dispatcher or some more or less arbitrary mechanism. In reality the "initial distribution" of resources is the result of all decisions and all activities that human beings have previously made.

14 One can find, for instance, an illustration of this idea about what are called "public goods". According to the theory of public goods, one can increase the well-being of at least a portion of individuals, without diminishing the welfare of any of them, by using a public production rather than by letting the "market" determine the quantities produced and the price of this good. But this theory is itself questionable (see Chapter 6).

15 In reality, the traditional theory of competition cannot bring such an evidence. In fact, capitalism can be defined as a system of private property. But neither the theory of pure and perfect competition nor the theory of general equilibrium are based on any specific assumption concerning property rights. This is the reason they can serve as a foundation both for central planning in collectivist economies and for the hypothetical description of market economies.

16 We encounter here an illustration of the serious methodological confusion from which economic science is suffering. The mathematical aspect of a theory is often considered as sufficient to found its scientific nature, although it depends on the nature of the reasoning process (which can be expressed through mathematics, English, French, Chinese, Morse code or Braille . . .).

2 Breaches of atomistic competition

The traditional theory of competition we have investigated has selected an approach to competition quite different from that of common sense, and this difference in the meaning of concepts is strange. This theory presupposes that entrepreneurs do not care about the behaviour of other producers, those who are commonly known as 'competitors'. They adjust to the 'market price' by using techniques and production processes that are freely available and used by all. If one adheres to such an approach to competition, one therefore considers naturally as noncompetitive a situation in which producers behave differently, regardless of the reason. More precisely, one considers generally that situations are noncompetitive when any of the conditions assumed to be necessary for pure and perfect competition are lacking. This is the case, in particular, with a monopoly (single producer) or an oligopoly (a small number of producers). In such cases one would then no longer be in a situation of economic optimum and therefore it becomes necessary to look to what extent it is possible to introduce the necessary conditions for pure and perfect competition – or, at least, its imitation.

Monopoly

A monopoly situation is defined simply in the traditional theory as a situation where there is a single producer in a given market: a situation in which the essential condition that makes atomistic competition possible is not satisfied.[1] What are the implications of this difference in market situations?

When there are a very large number of producers in a market, none of them can influence it. In particular, the selling price remains the same, regardless of the decisions taken by a particular producer. This is obviously not true in the case of a single producer. As the quantity demanded of a good changes in a direction opposite to that of a change of price, an increase in the quantity sold by a monopolist producer implies a decline in price. A monopolist necessarily becomes aware of this situation, and even if he or she does not have perfect knowledge of the demand curve, he or she can assess by experience, through a process of trial and error, the reactions of demand to changes in supply.

Let us represent graphically the behaviour of a monopolist on some market. For the sake of comparison, let us recall that, in the case of pure and perfect competition, the demand curve to the firm was horizontal (as we had represented in Figure 1.3).

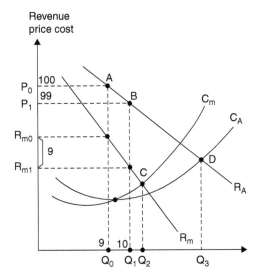

Figure 2.1

Figure 2.1 now represents a monopoly situation: the demand curve to the firm merges with the global demand curve for the whole market. This is the curve R_A (or average revenue curve), which indicates the sale price of one unit of goods (average revenue) for each quantity sold. Now, let us assume that the monopolist is, at a given time, at point A where he or she sells a quantity Q_0, for instance nine units of the product produced, at the maximum price per unit P_0 (= £100). The monopolist wonders whether it is worthwhile to increase the production by one unit – to sell ten units instead of nine. If sales increase, he or she shifts from point A to point B. The unit price will go down (from £100 to £99) in order to enable a greater production to be sold. Average revenue – the unit selling price – decreases by a value equal to one (100–99). However, it is not only the tenth unit that must now sell at the new price of £99, but the nine other units that were previously sold at a price of £100. Therefore, the variation of the total income is the result of a double effect:

- An increase of revenue equal to £99 corresponding to what is brought in by the tenth unit sold
- A decrease of revenues for each of the other nine units which are no more sold at a price of £100, but at a price of £99, which represents a decrease in revenues equal to £9

Finally, therefore, the marginal revenue – the additional revenue received when shifting from nine to ten units – is equal to £90.

The marginal revenue therefore decreases more quickly than the average revenue: the first decreases by £9 between A and B and the second by £1. The marginal revenue curve (R_m) is necessarily located below the average revenue curve (R_A).

When representing the atomistic competition situation, there was no need to distinguish between average revenue and marginal revenue. Indeed, the price – the unit revenue – was constant, regardless of the scale of production of a particular firm. In other words, the average revenue was constant, as was the marginal revenue, so that the average revenue curve and the marginal revenue curve were the same.

The monopolist does not behave differently from the producer in atomistic competition. Both seek to maximise their profit, but they are in different situations which mean their marginal revenue curves are different. The maximization of profit implies that the producer increases his production to the point where the marginal revenue is just equal to the marginal cost: This is point C in Figure 2.1, in the case of a monopolist. Indeed, if the monopolist produced more, the marginal revenue obtained would be less than his marginal cost. This does not necessarily mean that there would be losses, but it would certainly mean that additional units produced beyond this point would cost more than they would bring. The profit would therefore be decreasing as much. And if the producer steadily increased production, he or she would necessarily reach a point (D on Figure 2.1) where the average revenue would be equal to the average cost: where, that is, the profit would be zero. Beyond this point (if the production was greater than the quantity Q_3) profit would become negative.

Can we compare the situation of atomistic competition and the monopoly situation? The answer is yes from the point of view of the traditional theory. Indeed, let us assume that there is a single technique to produce a good, and that it is perfectly accessible to any producer. This assumption implies also that (average or marginal) cost curves are the same for all producers. In other words, if one was to substitute one single firm for two existing firms, the cost curves of the new single firm would be obtained by aggregation of the cost curves of the two previous firms. This is what is done in Figure 2.2: On the left quadrant one represents the

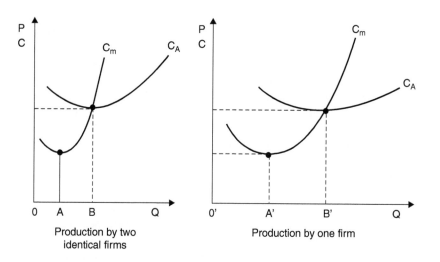

Production by two
identical firms

Production by one firm

Figure 2.2

marginal cost curve (C_m) and the average cost curve (C_A) for a firm, when there are two firms. These curves are assumed to be the same for both firms regardless of the firm one is considering. On the right are represented the aggregated curves of the two firms; one obtains the cost curves of the single firm which replaces them. Thus O'A' = 2OA and O'B' = 2OB. In the same way, if there were many firms, and if a single firm was substituted for them, the cost curves of the new single firm would be obtained by aggregation of the curves of the firms that it has replaced.

This representation properly takes into account the characteristics of the traditional monopoly theory, since it assumes that the only difference between a situation of competition and a monopoly situation comes from the number of firms and not from technical features of the production processes, which would be different in all the firms. Sometimes, however, it is assumed that the unit costs of production (average or marginal) vary depending on the size of the firm. In such a case one says that there are economies of scale, if unit costs are lower with greater production scale. But we must carefully distinguish this hypothesis from the one that is included in the traditional theory of monopoly. This traditional theory does not state technical differences brought about by the dimension of firms, depending on whether there is (atomistic) competition or monopoly. The traditional theory aims at showing that the state of the market is different under both assumptions (competition or monopoly) because of a different behaviour of producers in these different institutional environments. And these differences are themselves due to differences in information.

Indeed, the revenue curve the entrepreneur faces is not necessarily the curve of the overall revenue on the market, but the specific revenue curve for the demand addressed to him or her. In the case of atomistic competition there is therefore a discrepancy between the aggregate demand and the demand to the firm, whereas the monopolist is perfectly aware of the aggregate demand curve, which is also the curve for the demand that is addressed to the monopoly firm. This specific knowledge gives to him or her a particular power on the market.

Let us, indeed, consider again the curves of Figure 2.2 and let us bring them into Figure 2.3, assuming now that the left quadrant of the figure represents a firm in a situation of competition and that there is a very large number (n) of firms, all identical, in the studied sector of production. Let us assume that there has been a period during which there was a relatively small number of firms, that the market price was equal to P_0 and firms were then placed in A (equalization of the marginal cost and the market price), which allowed them to obtain a profit (since the average cost was lower than the market price). The existence of this profit has attracted new (identical) firms and, gradually, the market price has declined until it has reached P_1, so that firms were placed at point B where profit is zero (the average cost is equal to the selling price). Now let us look, on the right side of Figure 2.3, at what is happening in the case of a monopoly. The point that would correspond to the longterm equilibrium of the competitive situation would be point B', but the monopolist is not interested in being at this point, because he or she would then have a zero profit. In the monopolist's continuous efforts to adapt to the market, it is in his or her best interest to stop the growth of production at a lower level,

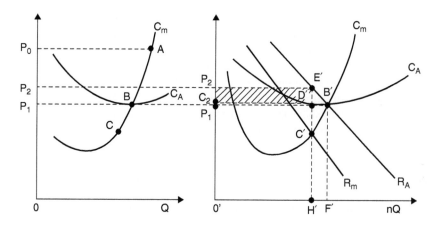

Figure 2.3

that is, to choose the point C'. Now, the monopolist can do so because he or she is the only producer of the concerned good. The monopolist can therefore decide independently the total quantity of goods that is delivered to the market.

It can easily be seen in Figure 2.3 that the monopolist has an interest in making supply scarcer in the market (than in the case of competition), so as to maximise his profit. If he or she chooses point C', the unit cost of production (average cost) is equal to C_2 (i.e. H'D'), but the unit selling price – that is, the average revenue – is equal to P_2 (= H'E'). The profit per sold unit is thus equal to D'E', and total profit is equal to the surface of the hatched rectangle: the product of the unit profit times the number of units sold. This rectangle has a maximum area when the marginal revenue and the marginal cost are equal. In fact, any additional production would give the monopolist an additional revenue lower than the additional cost so that total profit would decrease.

One could obviously wonder why producers in competition could not arrive at the same result; why they would not move, all of them, to point C and ask a price P_2. The reason this is not possible is simple: It is because they all *compete with* each other. Let us suppose in fact that competing producers are located, at a given time, at point C, which allows them to ask a price P_2 for the production of all producers. Each producer understands that he or she can make an additional profit in trying to increase market share, since the marginal cost is lower than the selling price that each producer considers as immutable (and which is equal to the average selling price). But the effort of each producer to try to increase market share increases the total supply and lowers the price. The phenomenon ceases when all have arrived at point B, where they have no more interest in pursuing this ruinous competition. This is in some sense the paradox of the traditional theory of competition: The search for profit by all participants in the market leads to a cancellation of profits. In this game the winners are consumers, since they get the lowest possible price, which also induces them to buy more than they would in other circumstances. The traditional theory of competition and monopoly then

leads to a normative statement: that consumers have an interest in atomistic competition, and that they are 'despoiled' by monopolies. Monopolies, indeed, cause
an 'artificial' scarcity of goods on markets so as to get more profits. Compared
with the situation of atomistic competition, a monopoly would get what is called
a '*superprofit*'. We therefore find again the traditional idea, that atomistic competition leads to a 'social optimum'.[2] It then plays the role of a 'norm', the rate
of profit of the situation of pure and perfect competition being called a *normal*
profit and any profit above this norm being called a 'superprofit' (but let us recall
it again, strangely enough the 'normal profit' is zero . . .).

The above reasonings, and the consequences that are drawn from them, seem
unanswerable. They seem to justify all the laws and regulations designed to fight
against monopolies and to introduce (pure and perfect) competition – at least, they
seem to oblige monopolies to behave as if competition was prevailing. However,
we shall see later on that these arguments raise many problems and are debatable.

Oligopoly

So far we have considered two possible situations, one in which there is a very
large number of producers for a product (atomistic competition) and one in which
there is only one producer (monopoly). We now consider the case in which there
is a small number of producers. The consequences of this market structure will
depend on the ability of producers to organise themselves in order to obtain some
power on the market, as do monopolists.

There is something of a paradox in the theory of atomistic competition. Indeed,
what motivates producers is only the profit motive. It is to get profit that they
enter into a market where there is an opportunity for gain. But, each behaving
in the same way, their common pursuit of profit eventually kills profits. Only the
monopolist succeeds in keeping it, because he or she creates a scarcity of supply
in the market. We already wondered whether producers in competition could not
behave in the same way: that is, act in such a way that they could stay at a point
such as C in Figure 2.3. If they are very numerous, their numbers prevent it, since
it is difficult for them to get an agreement and, if ever an agreement could have
been reached, some of the participants in the agreement would likely be doing free
riding, trying to increase their market share. But what can happen in an oligopoly
situation?

To get a profit comparable to that of the monopolist, producers in an oligopoly
must reconcile their tendency to compete with the gain they could get by behaving as if they were in a situation of monopoly and thus avoiding competition. The
most profitable behaviour for them consists therefore in maximizing the common
profit at point H' (Figure 2.3) by creating a scarcity of supply and distributing
the common profit thus obtained. When producers in an oligopoly succeed in an
agreement of this kind, one says that there is a cartel agreement. It is supposed
to be designed to create a monopolistic situation even though there are several
producers.

The sensitive issue is clearly that of the distribution of the common profit. It
can result from *a priori* rules or from discretionary negotiations. In either case a

control procedure is necessary to check that the cartel members comply with the decisions taken in common and to punish potential deviations.

Let us compare the behaviour of producers participating in a cartel agreement and that of the monopoly. We have seen that monopolists have an interest in being at point H' (in Figure 2.3). If they have perfect knowledge of the characteristics of demand, they decide a sale price P_2 and know that they will sell a quantity O'H'. Of course, in reality, this perfect information does not exist and it is through a process of trial and error and through guesses that they will determine little by little the price that appears to be optimal.

The members of a cartel can certainly have diverging views about the market and a procedure for determining the joint action and the common price is there-fore necessary. However, we will assume for simplicity that they are in the same situation as monopolists from the point of view of information. Anyway, the most crucial problem is probably that of the distribution of market shares among the members. Let us suppose that all the cartel members manage to agree to sell at a price P_2.

They know that together they will sell O'H'. But at that price there is a 'super-profit' equal to D'E' (per unit of product). Let us assume for the sake of simplicity that all the members of the cartel have exactly the same cost curves[3] and that it has been decided that all will sell the same amount, namely O'H'/n (if n is the number of participants). Each member of the cartel has in fact interest in climbing on its marginal cost curve from point C', since there is a possibility of gain. Members will actually do so if they think that the other members of the cartel will respect the cartel agreement, which means that the sale price will remain close to P_2, even if such members have increased their individual market share. Admittedly, unlike what was assumed in a situation of atomistic competition, the fluctuations of each member's production have a visible impact on the whole production of the cartel and therefore on the sale price, but it can be assumed that this influence is relatively small if there are enough members in the cartel. In other words, it is in the interest of each producer that the others respect the agreement, but each member individually has no interest in respecting it. Of course, if no producer respects the cartel agreement, it will be ineffective and there will be a similar situ-ation to that of atomistic competition, that is a sale price equal to P_1: Buyers will be at the optimum, but producers will have a zero profit. The effectiveness of a cartel depends essentially on the efficiency of the procedures devised to discipline members. This is why we can say that the cartel is an unstable structure and that, furthermore, there cannot exist a single theory to describe the behaviour of the members of the cartel and the market situation that results, since it depends on the specific circumstances of collective decisions and controls. One can, at best, only draw up a catalogue of the possible modes of organisation of a cartel. We know in any case that the cartel *can* behave as a monopoly.[4]

Economic optimum in the absence of atomistic competition

Atomistic competition – as we have seen – leads to points such as B and B' in Figure 2.3. This position is considered by the traditional theory of competition as *optimal*, in the sense that nobody can obtain an additional gain without a single one among others having to bear a loss. The cartel leads to points D' and E' (lower quantity, higher price and therefore higher profit). When shifting from a situation of atomistic competition to a cartel situation, there is a gain for producers and a loss for consumers.[5] Therefore, there is basically no way to compare the two situations. Indeed, it is impossible to quantify the benefits drawn by individuals from their own activities and there is therefore no way to compare them. In other words, one cannot say that the extra gain obtained by producers organised as a cartel *offsets* (or even overcompensates) the losses incurred by consumers: Those who get the gains and the losses are not the same.

It remains no less true that in the entire area bounded by points D'E'B' there are opportunities of gain when leaving the position D'E' and coming closer to B'. In fact, the possible price per unit of product (average revenue) is everywhere higher than the unit cost of production (average cost). One could therefore imagine that producers and consumers agree to obtain together this global potential earning and to distribute it among them in one way or another. Let us thus imagine that buyers also organise themselves to constitute a cartel in order to coordinate their actions and to negotiate the price of the product. We may then talk of a bilateral cartel (a situation in which both producers and buyers are organised as cartels).

Figure 2.4, which incorporates the characteristics of Figure 2.3, gives an illustration of this situation. In fact, let us assume that one moves from a production O'H' to a production O'F', therefore from a price P_2 to a price P_1. In the total of sales made by the members of the cartel of sellers (O'F'), one can distinguish the part that was sold in a situation of cartel of sellers (before bargaining with buyers) and the additional part which is now sold in a situation of bilateral cartel, that is, as a consequence of the negotiation with the buyers, which leads to the point of

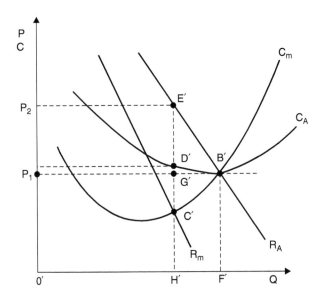

Figure 2.4

atomistic competition (B'). As regards the part O'H' there is a transfer from the sellers to the buyers: this part, which was sold at price P_2 is now sold at price P_1, meaning that the rectangle $P_2P_1G'E'$ represents the total amount of revenue lost by the cartel of sellers and the total gain achieved by the buyers thanks to their cartel organization. But let us imagine that buyers agree to give back all of this rectangle to the suppliers. The situation would be, from the point of view of the part O'H' of transactions on this product, exactly the same as in the case of a cartel of sellers.

But the fact remains that there is a net gain for the additional part of transactions: H'F'. This gain is represented by the triangle E'G'B'. In fact, if one starts from the level of transactions H' and gets closer to F', any additional unit purchased provides to buyers a supplement of satisfaction that is for them at least equal to the satisfaction they could have obtained by buying another good at a price identical to the price at which they have purchased the unit in question (otherwise they would have not bought it). Triangle E'G'B' therefore represents the maximum value in market price that they could ultimately abandon without a decrease in welfare. In other words, if buyers – organised in a cartel – were to abandon to suppliers the rectangle $P_2P_1G'E'$, buyers and suppliers would be exactly in the same situation as the one in which only producers are organised as a cartel. To encourage suppliers to accept the price P_1, buyers may then be tempted to abandon to them a portion of the value of the triangle E'G'B'.

This means that shifting from the situation in which production has been made scarce (H') to a situation expected to be similar to that of atomistic competition, there is a net 'social gain'. This gain is measured – in terms of market prices – by the area of the triangle E'G'B'. A negotiation about the sharing of this gain allows all market participants to be in a better situation than in the situation of a relative scarcity of production.

One can find in the so-called theory of welfare an idea often called the 'Kaldor-Hicks compensation principle', according to the names of the two economists who have stated it. According to this principle, it would be sufficient that compensation be possible between potential winners and potential losers for a comparison between two situations to be done, although the shift from one situation to the other would involve gains for some and losses for others. Thus, one could consider that a change of situation has led to an optimum if the gains are greater than the losses, even if the compensation is not actually performed. Yet, if the compensation is not actually done, the loss of some remains and no criterion can state that it has a 'value' inferior to the gains made by others. For a situation to be considered as better than another, it must be *effectively* chosen by those involved without using any coercion. Indeed, there is no way to assess the subjective value of this loss as long as it has not been the subject of an exchange process.

The possibility of a shift to point B' therefore results, of course, from the ability of buyers to organise into a cartel. The difficulties they encounter for this are obviously symmetrical to those faced by producers in the creation of a cartel. If buyers are very numerous, none of them will find interest in taking time and spending resources to organise the cartel of buyers. Furthermore, the procedures needed to implement a redistribution from buyers to producers (to induce them to go to B') are necessarily costly and uncertain. Therefore, compensation may not take place.

Let us imagine, however, that buyers are few. They can then organise a cartel and they may wish to compensate sellers for the loss they incur when going from E'D' to B'. This is to say, the compensation principle is devoid of scope if it is stated independently of the concrete situations of the market. Why should one say that a situation A is better than a situation B because those who lose in the eventual transition from B to A *could* be compensated, if the behaviour of all – taking into account market conditions – is such that there is no chance that the losers actually get a compensation?

If one takes as reference a situation of atomistic competition, one must therefore admit that a monopoly or a cartel lead to 'suboptimal' situations, which would justify an intervention either to eliminate or to avoid the supposed bad consequences of this state of affairs. But we will see later that this conclusion must be modified if one adopts another – more realistic – approach to competition.

Notes

1 Symmetrically one calls 'monopsony' a situation in which there is a single buyer on a market.
2 It remains true, however, that the concept of optimum should be used with caution, because, when comparing atomistic competition and a monopoly situation, everyone wins from shifting from a monopoly situation to atomistic competition, except the monopolist.
3 The nature of the reasoning would not be changed if it were assumed that the cost curves were different, but it would be a little more complicated, and the procedure for disciplining the members of the cartel would also be somewhat more complex.
4 At least if it is assumed that the economic calculation of producers is made in the same way in both cases. This assumption is obviously questionable insofar as any economic calculation is subjective and as the members of a hypothetical cartel and the owners of a hypothetical monopoly are not the same individuals.
5 This was the case, for example, when the relatively competitive oil market became cartelised in 1974 by the creation of the oil cartel OPEC.

3 A critical appraisal of the atomistic theory

The theory of pure and perfect competition – or atomistic competition – and the theory of monopoly are formally correct theories, in the sense that they unfold logically once their basic assumptions have been settled. But there is a fundamental problem, namely that of the relevance of these assumptions for the understanding of the world as it is in reality. One may wonder, from this point of view, whether there is a need to retain one or the other of the characteristics that are considered constitutive of a competitive situation. But more deeply, the traditional theories we have met assume – often in an implicit way – specific behaviours of existing or potential producers. However, it is legitimate to think, as we will see, that they do not behave according to the traditional model.

A critical review of the assumptions of the model of pure and perfect competition

Obsessed by the desire to define a producer who would be unable to have any influence on a market, the traditional theory sets a number of conditions considered as necessary for such an aim. There is pure and perfect competition on a market if there are many producers, producing a homogeneous and divisible good and benefiting from perfect information. A market can be defined as an abstract place on which a good is traded. As soon as a good is defined, one can therefore define a market.[1] This is why one describes a market from the characteristics of the concerned good: one will say, for instance, that the market is a market of pure and perfect competition if the goods that are sold are homogeneous, divisible, and produced by countless producers, using freely available information.

As we have already seen, the definition of a homogeneous product – and therefore of the corresponding market – is extremely arbitrary. As one adopts a more or less precise definition of a good, this good will appear as homogeneous or heterogeneous. Thus, arabica coffee from Harrar sold by a given shop in Paris, obtained from a specific wholesaler, at one time, is probably a homogeneous product (and perceived as such by its potential buyers), but its market is obviously not a 'pure and perfect' competitive market, since there is a single supplier. At another extreme, one will obviously notice that there are a large number of sellers of 'raw materials for hot drinks', but the product thus defined will not be homogeneous (coffee, chocolate, ground coffee, coffee beans, arabica or robusta, mixtures, etc.). Now, there is no way to decide *a priori* whether one should choose the narrower or the more extensive definition. Thus, by arbitrarily choosing one definition or another, one can say that competition exists or does not exist on a market. Therefore, what may be the utility of a theory that can be used only in a perfectly arbitrary way? It is zero.

Now, looking at the other constituent elements of 'pure and perfect competition' only reinforces this conclusion. Thus, what may be the interest of the assumption according to which there are many producers (and therefore an infinite supply elasticity)? It certainly helps to stylise in a very specific manner the behaviour of producers by setting a limit case. But this assumption is very far from the reality of markets and therefore from the actual behaviour of producers. Similarly the assumption of perfect information is a limited and unrealistic assumption and it is therefore deprived of any interest (except as a step in reasoning that helps to gradually define the characteristics of a model). Information, in fact, is necessarily a scarce good. Each individual is looking for the information that is optimal for him or her, and each individual therefore bears the corresponding costs. Because of the diversity of human beings, it is inconceivable that two entrepreneurs may have – or rather may want – exactly the same set of information at the same time.

The ideal entrepreneur of the traditional model of pure and perfect competition is designed to be exactly like other ones. Such ideal entrepreneurs are organisers of production factors in a world of perfect information: there is only one combination of factors and techniques to produce a given homogeneous good, the 'entrepreneurs' know it, and they apply it mechanically. We have seen that the theory of pure and perfect competition leads to the crucial conclusion that the rate of profit is zero when *equilibrium* prevails. But this equilibrium corresponds to a predetermined state where, at the limit, any human decision is discharged: to produce any good there would be, in a sort of definitive way, a single technique that could be considered as the best of all. This technique would have emerged independently of the decisions of those who implement it and it would be optimal from a technical point of view (while, from an economic point of view, optimality corresponds to a preference among several possibilities). If by chance a producer was in a different situation and was temporarily using a technique less profitable than the most efficient one, he or she would quickly converge toward the common situation since information is perfect, that is, it is available at a zero price.

The theory of pure and perfect competition is therefore based on a mechanical vision of life (perfect information, technical approach to economic problems). It is then not surprising that it leads to the idea that the profit rate becomes nil. But what becomes nil in reality is something that has nothing to do with profit. In fact, profit has a specific nature. In a situation where there is uncertainty, that is, a situation in which information is not perfect, someone has to take care of risks. Now, let us consider the case where several people must cooperate for the implementation of an activity. One can give the name of 'firm' to this cooperative organisation and the firm can be defined as a set of contracts. However, given the diversity of skills and aims of participants in this abstract reality that is a firm, it is normal that the contracts between the participants be differentiated. Some contracts will promise a given payment to the signatories of these contracts for their contribution to the common productive effort. This will be the case of wages and interest payments, which are certain incomes. Other individuals will receive an uncertain income and this is precisely the case of profits. The profit can be defined as a *residual income* in situations of uncertainty. It is positive only if the value of the product made by the joint activity is not exhausted by the payment of all the incomes which have been promised as certain by contract. Insofar as risks exist necessarily, someone has to take them in charge. The entrepreneur – or, more precisely, the capitalist – is the one who must play this role. It is he or she who takes decisions concerning the production processes because the entrepreneur is the only one to have a residual remuneration, that is, an income that does not depend on what could be promised by contract, but on the quality of his or her own decisions. The profit pays responsibility. It is clear then why the traditional theory of competition is wrong. It claims to explain competition among entrepreneurs who are not real entrepreneurs; one might even say that they have no existence. The basic conclusion of the traditional theory of competition – that the profit becomes nil – is already contained in the initial assumptions, since profit is the remuneration of risk taking and responsibility and the model of pure and perfect competition requires perfect information, that is, the absence of risk. The future is assumed to be perfectly known and it is why no one can differentiate him- or herself from the others. Assuming that pure and perfect competition prevails in all activities – or, at least, where it may not exist, policies are implemented to force people to behave as if it existed, that is, in order to get a zero profit – nobody has a reason to move toward one activity rather than another. The allocation of 'entrepreneurs'[2] in this world of 'pure and perfect' competition may arise either from a random process or from a decision of some central planner, but certainly not from individual decisions of people who would be looking for a 'profit'.

According to the traditional theory, the situation of pure and perfect competition corresponds to an optimum because the benefit is nil – so that, therefore, no one can obtain an improvement of his or her fate without a decrease of the fate of someone else. The profit of the monopolist is then called a superprofit because it can only result, according to the supporters of the theory of pure and perfect competition, from the despoilment of the buyers: there is a superprofit only in comparison to a standard of zero profit. Therefore, the profit is either zero – in the case of competition – or it is positive – in the case of the monopoly – but in no case it is linked to the function of risk taking which is yet characteristic of the entrepreneur. The theory of pure and perfect competition and its corollary, the theory of monopoly, are therefore constructed by discharging what is the essence of markets, that is, the existence of entrepreneurs.

In a situation of perfect information there is equalization of the rates of remuneration in all activities and for all firms, whether it is the remuneration of capital or labour. A particular form of work is that of the pseudo-entrepreneur of the traditional theory, whose only role is to implement the production processes that are 'given' to him or her, which are determined exogenously, without such an individual's incentives and decisions, which may have no role to play. Therefore this remuneration is wrongly called a 'profit'. Because this individual has the official title of entrepreneur, his or her remuneration is not called a wage but a profit. In fact, in this theory, the pseudo-entrepreneur is paid for the work he or she provides, like any employee. Insofar as the pseudo-entrepreneur is also an owner of capital or of a part of the capital, he or she may be paid as such, but this part of the remuneration is more akin to an interest than to a profit. In fact, in the world of perfect information where one is supposed to be, there is equalization of the rates of return on capital in all its uses. The owner of capital knows with certainty that this capital will bring in a certain amount for each period. It is then exactly the same to hold financial claims (e.g., bonds) or to hold property rights in the firm. Therefore, saying that profit is zero does not mean that the 'entrepreneur' is deprived of any remuneration, but simply that he or she receives a wage and an interest for the work and capital he or she has provided to the firm.

The entrepreneur of the traditional theory is therefore no more an entrepreneur than the bureaucrat who runs a factory in a centralised and planned society where property rights are not individualised. In this sense, the traditional theory of competition should be used to describe an economy similar to the Soviet economy and not an economy of individual property rights. In a centralised society of this kind, in fact, the production is not considered from an economic point of view – i.e. from the point of view of the aims, incentives and actions of human beings – but from a technical point of view. At one given time there is a single production process to produce a good and one can calculate a cost in a way supposedly objective, i.e. independent from the one who is making calculations or who decides. The central planner can then impose the adoption of the same process of production and the same plant overall the territory he is controlling. Everyone has the same costs, and of course, the profit does not exist in principle. Certainly, the inevitable uncertainties lead to negative or positive accounting results, but the fact remains that the fundamental principle for the working of a social organisation of this type – its ideal somehow – corresponds exactly to what the traditional theory claims to be the model of competition: In the more or less long term, all firms converge towards a similar situation where the marginal cost is equal to the sale price and where profit is zero. The lack of differentiation between producers is the characteristic of a 'pure and perfect' planned economy, as it is in the traditional theory of 'pure and perfect' competition. Thus, the standard by which one assesses competition in the atomistic theory is its greater or lesser similarity with a planned economy!

If the pure and perfect competition model does not correspond absolutely to a correct analysis of the world as it is, what could be concluded? One can force the world to conform to the model or one can modify the model. This later possibility is what we will see later on, but first we need to revisit the concept of 'superprofit'.

A critical review of the concept of superprofit

There is in the traditional theory two symmetric situations: competition, characterised by the existence of a very large number of producers getting a profit, and monopoly or oligopoly, characterised by the existence of a small number of producers (possibly one) getting a 'superprofit'. But let us refer again to Figure 2.4. It is undeniable that the monopolist has interest to produce only O'H'. It is a superprofit compared with the situation of reference B' where he would equalise the average cost and the average revenue, which means that his profit would be zero. But perhaps one should wonder about the conditions enabling him to stay on points E'D'.

If the production is made scarcer, the monopolist producing only the amount O'H', a critical issue needs to be raised. In fact, there are in this case unexploited opportunities for profits, because, by expanding production from O'H', 'one' could get profits, the profit becoming zero only for the amount of production O'F'. Certainly, it is not in the interest of the monopolist to produce this quantity, at least in the circumstances in which he or she is placed. But can it happen that, in other circumstances – that is, with a different set of assumptions – the monopolist may be induced to produce the amount O'F'? Or that others might be tempted by the possibility of obtaining a profit? In other words, one can start from the simple observation that, whenever there is an opportunity of profit, there are normally people noticing and exploiting it.[3]

Truly, it is this idea we have already met (in Chapter 2) when we discussed the possibility that buyers negotiate with sellers and encourage them to move to B' by giving back to them a part of the surplus that they could thus obtain. We had seen that the realization of this assumption was based on the existence of specific conditions. But when the negotiation is between a monopolist (single seller) and a monopsonist (single buyer) – that is, when there is what is called a *bilateral monopoly* – one can easily imagine that they understand the interest that they may get by maximizing their overall profit and distributing it in a satisfactory way for both, compared to any other possible situation. But there are other cases in which, despite the existence of a monopolist, the production can be done at the same point as in a situation of competition, that is, at point B'.

The first situation we can imagine is that where the monopolist exploits these possibilities of profit. In fact, we started with the implicit assumption that the price should necessarily be the same for the product a monopolist sells anywhere on the market. It follows that, if he or she plans to increase the quantity produced and sold, the monopolist must reduce the sale price not only for the additional units he or she plans to sell, but also for all other units: those sold earlier at a higher price (and this is the reason why the marginal revenue curve is below the average revenue curve).

But let us suppose that the monopolist can make price discriminations, meaning that every unit can be sold at a different price. Imagine also that, at some time and for some reason, the quantity OH (Figure 3.1) is sold priced at P_2. We know that in the absence of price discrimination the monopolist has no interest in going further. But if price discrimination is possible, he or she may decide to sell an additional unit at price P_3, so as to expand the selling opportunities without having to diminish the price of the previous units. On the additional unit, HL, an additional profit is obtained which is given by the difference between P_3 and the marginal cost, C_3, whereas the profit on the units previously sold is not affected. The monopolist will thus continue until the point M, going down on the average revenue curve, and the point R, going up on the marginal cost curve, merge with point B. The total profit of the monopolist is equal to the sum, on the one hand, of the maximum profit that

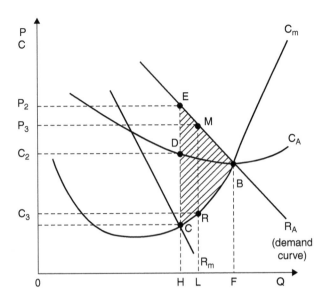

Figure 3.1

can be made in the absence of discrimination, which is given by the size of the rectangle P_2EDC_2 (similar to the one of Figure 2.4), and, on the other hand, of the amount of the profit due to discrimination, which corresponds to the area bounded by the points CEB (i.e. the shaded area of Figure 3.1).

In the case we are investigating, we have assumed that the monopolist practiced a policy of discrimination only from a level of sales equal to OH. But if he can practice it from the first unit sold, his total income is even greater, since it is equal to the whole surface of the area between the marginal cost curve and the average revenue curve (the maximum quantity produced being equal to OF, corresponding to point B).[4]

In this case, therefore, the level of production is exactly the same as in pure and perfect competition (assuming that firms have exactly the same cost curves in either case). But, however, an important difference remains between both situations. In fact, the monopolist appropriates the whole consumer surplus: all the gain that buyers would get through the decline in selling prices. In a situation of pure and perfect competition, if the price decreases, for instance, from P_2 to P_3 for all purchased units, consumers make a gain since they agreed to pay the price P_2 for the quantity OH and they can now get it at a lower price, P_3 (and, because of this price drop, they also purchase a quantity greater than OH). It is this gain that is called the consumer surplus. Graphically, it is represented by the area located between the average revenue curve (which is the demand curve) and the horizontal line of price, for example P_3M: The more the price decreases the more the consumer surplus increases and the more consumers are satisfied – except, of course, if this surplus is confiscated. This is precisely what a discriminating monopoly can do. A discriminating monopoly is therefore able to appropriate all of the surplus, while there was a sharing of the surplus between the buyer and the seller in the case of a bilateral monopoly.

When producers are able to do price discrimination it is sometimes called a dumping policy, although this term is most often used for the cases where price discrimination is made according to countries.[5] It is obvious that the possibilities of price discrimination are relatively rare. They imply that those who buy at a certain price cannot resell to those who buy at a higher price. This is so, in particular, for personal services where the price depends on the specific characteristics of clients.

Gerald O'Driscoll[6] stresses that, if there are untapped potential gains, one reason may be that, in order to get these gains, one would have to bear additional costs that are not considered in accounting. One then has the impression that there is underproduction and superprofit, but if one produced more than OH (Figure 3.1) the marginal profit would actually be negative. A particular example of this situation can be precisely the situation we just saw, namely that of discrimination. One can probably always imagine methods for discriminating prices according to buyers. But these methods are not free. As is the case with any production, it is legitimate to assume that the production costs of the methods of discrimination are increasing.

Let us represent this situation in Figure 3.2 (inspired by a figure of Gerald O'Driscoll). It has been assumed for the sake of simplicity that the marginal cost curve is horizontal, that is, that the marginal costs are constant, regardless of the scale of production. This curve is then obviously exactly the same as the average cost curve. According to the traditional theory of monopoly, the monopolist

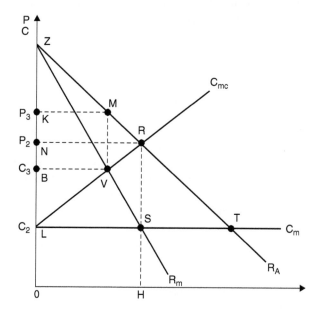

Figure 3.2

produces the amount OH that he sells at a price P_2. His marginal or average profit per unit is equal to RS and his total profit, which is at a maximum for a production OH, is equal to the area of the rectangle NLSR. The consumer surplus is equal to ZNR and there is a potential untapped gain equal to the area of the triangle RST. In a situation of pure and perfect competition one would produce at point T, the profit of the producers would be zero (since the selling price would be equal to C_2) and the consumer surplus would be equal to the triangle ZLT. Now, the marginal cost, C_m, does takes into account only material production costs, but not, for example, the costs of researching buyers and the possible ways to discriminate between them (costs of information and exclusion). One should therefore distinguish between two curves: on the one hand, the curve C_m that corresponds to the costs incurred for the production of a product, which we assumed to be horizontal (constant costs), and, on the other hand, the curve C_{mc} that adds to the costs of production the costs which have to be borne in order to make the product in question available for different buyers. Now, we may assume that these costs are increasing with the amount of sales, which determines the shape of the curve C_{mc}. This curve C_{mc} can correspond to two different situations:

- It may come from the existence of costs incurred to find a market, totally independent from the structure of the market. Thus, one will first meet an urban demand close to the places of production, and then meet more and more distant and disseminated demands. These costs are identical whether there is a monopoly or atomistic competition. But the market equilibrium point will be different in the two cases. If there is atomistic competition, the equilibrium will be in R, the consumer surplus will be equal to ZRN and the surplus of producers to NRL. In the case of a non discriminating monopoly the equilibrium will be in V (with a price P_3 and a production cost C_3); the consumer surplus will be reduced to ZKM and the gain of the producer will be higher, since it will be equal to the sum of the surplus LBV and of the 'superprofit', KMVB. In all cases, the point T – which appeared as the point of equilibrium in the case of atomistic competition – is purely fictitious: It does not take into account a portion of the costs.
- If the difference between C_{mc} and C_m is only caused by the costs of discrimination, C_{mc} can describe only the behaviour of a discriminating monopoly and not the one of producers in atomistic competition or in a nondiscriminating monopoly. The discriminating monopolist will then go to point R, a point that 'looks like' the equilibrium point of atomistic competition, but which in fact corresponds to a very different situation. The surplus of buyers is reduced to zero and the monopolist gain is equal to the entire area ZLR. Indeed, the first unit costs C_2, but it is sold at a price equal to OZ, then the cost of each following unit increases according to the slope of C_{mc}, while the price moves along R_A.[7]

Why does the curve C_{mc} increase when there is discrimination? It is not expensive to find the first customer, willing to pay a high price: There is no cost of exclusion, since other potential customers exclude themselves simply because they do not wish to pay this high price. But exclusion becomes more and more costly, since it is necessary to prevent those who could pay a high price from paying a lower price. One can imagine that the seller proposes to his clients a conditional contract prohibiting resale by the buyer. While it may be easy to monitor compliance with the contract when there are a few big buyers, this is probably more expensive when a product is sold to many small buyers. To expand the market, the discriminating monopolist must therefore bear rising control costs.

Of course there may be both costs for making a product available on the market and costs of discrimination. Whatever the situation, the traditional teachings apply: if there are neither costs of delivery to markets nor costs of discrimination, the monopoly goes to point S (and gets a superprofit equal to NRSL), whereas atomistic competition would lead to point T. If there are delivery costs, the monopoly leads to point V (with a superprofit KMVB) and atomistic competition to point R. If discrimination is possible, it is impossible to compare the monopoly and atomistic competition, since only the monopoly is capable of doing price discrimination. It then moves to point R and gets all of the surplus both of the consumer and of the producer, namely the area of the triangle ZLD (which, it should be noted, is not necessarily greater than the superprofit of the nondiscriminating monopoly, which means that price discrimination is not necessarily profitable).

Thus it seems well established that (atomistic) competition is beneficial to consumers. However, the previous analysis must be complemented by looking at the processes that allow us to understand the genesis of the differences in market structures. This is what we will now study. We will see that the evaluations one can do concerning these various forms of markets are pretty deeply modified.

Notes

1 In reality, one cannot define a market from a single good. In fact, a market is the (abstract) place where a good is traded *against another good*. Thus, in a barter economy, we may mention the wheat/tomatoes market, i.e. the set of transactions which involve the exchange of wheat against tomatoes, or the wheat/salad market, shoes/peanuts market, etc . . . As we have already said, in our time, there is a 'generalised intermediary' in trade which is called 'money' so that, when one speaks, for instance, of the wheat market, in reality it implies the wheat/currency market, which is in fact the market for wheat against all other goods. It is essential not to forget this 'double' character of the market, for example, in macroeconomics. It is perhaps less necessary in the field which we are presently exploring, because we mainly focus on the production structure of a specific good.
2 It would be more correct to name these people "managers" and not "entrepreneurs".
3 This important remark is made by Gerald O'Driscoll (1982). This text has inspired some of the developments that follow.
4 Of course, such a situation is purely hypothetical since it assumes that the monopolist knows perfectly the reaction of each purchaser at each price.
5 For an analysis of international dumping one can refer to Chapter 10 of the present book.
6 O'Driscoll (1982).
7 The discriminating monopoly can avoid making the marginal revenue curve lower than the average revenue curve (which determines, in the absence of discrimination, an equilibrium at point V for a monopoly). In the case of discrimination, these two curves are indeed merged.

4 The entrepreneur and the dynamics of competition

We have made some progress in the comparison between atomistic competition and monopoly. Thus, we now know that the conditions in which entrepreneurs are working are not necessarily identical in both cases; certain monopolies can make a policy of price discrimination, which a producer in atomistic competition can never do. The fact remains that the monopolist can reach positions that are inaccessible for the producers in atomistic competition, because he or she has a certain control of the market. Thus, the monopolist may practise price discrimination or make production scarcer to increase the price. But we have also seen that one cannot be satisfied with the idea that the monopolist receives a superprofit. It may indeed happen that this superprofit is only apparent and that it is actually absorbed by costs that are usually not taken into account. But also and above all, we have not yet really answered the fundamental question: how can we explain that no one exploits the possibilities of gains which necessarily exist if there is a superprofit?

The freedom to enter a market

According to the atomistic theory of competition, *if there are* many producers, *at one given time*, for a given product, there is competition (and the profit rate – marginal and even average – becomes zero at equilibrium). But this theory does not worry at all about the processes through which a large number of producers could emerge and, symmetrically, about the factors that explain that there are no more producers when there is a monopoly or an oligopolistic situation.

Let us take again the example of the market for atomic power plants. Does it make sense to say that there is a small number of producers of nuclear power plants in a country and that, therefore, there is a superprofit, compared to a situation where there would be an infinite number of producers (or at least a great number)? To be sure, one may say that technical constraints preclude the coexistence of a large number of producers, but there is no competition in this case so that producers, making the most from this specificity, are in a position to impose on buyers a 'too high' price and a 'too low' quantity. But it is still necessary to wonder why some are settled in this market and not others. Let us imagine (simplifying the actual data of the problem) that a potential entrepreneur wonders whether he should produce wheat – which can be assumed to be sold on a 'competitive' market – or atomic power plants – assumed to be sold on a market of monopolist kind. If he chooses to produce atomic power plants is it because he can get a superprofit or because his personal specialisation gives him a comparative advantage for atomic power plants over wheat?

Let us imagine indeed that we can be at an initial point of time where no one is producing either wheat or atomic power plants, but where the technologies exist for both activities. There is also a very large number of potential producers who wonder about their choices of production. We know that there must be a small number of producers of nuclear power plants, while wheat producers can be countless. Those who decide to build atomic power plants do so obviously because, *from their own point of view*, the profit that they expect to get from this activity is higher than the one they can expect from wheat production. For them and for them only, this profit, which is necessarily anticipated and subjective, is a superprofit (compared to what they could get in the production of wheat). But, symmetrically, those who engage in the production of wheat rather than nuclear power plants, while the option was open to them, do so because, *for them*, the profit from the production of wheat is higher than the one they could get from the production of nuclear power plants. Each one acts in order to obtain a superprofit, which is purely subjective in nature. It may happen that some were misled and that they later regret their choice. But the fact remains that they have made their choices freely, from an evaluation of their own opportunities and of the potential markets they could be facing.

Now, it is likely that the business risk is higher in the construction of nuclear power plants than in the production of wheat. It is so precisely because, for technical reasons of indivisibility and possible saturation of the market, a very small number of producers can coexist on the market for nuclear power plants at a given time. Each of these producers must bear the risk that a more efficient competitor will appear one day, so that the technologies that the first producers had developed will become obsolete and they may be forced to leave the market. Their total profit will thus be reduced by the losses they will have to bear in such circumstances. It is therefore inappropriate to analyze the so-called superprofit by taking into account the fact that *at one point of time* the profit is higher than in other activities or higher than it would be if there were an infinite number of producers.

At the initial time we are considering, anyone can make the choice to become a producer of nuclear power plants. Only a few make this choice, others choosing to produce wheat. The reason is simple: They do not have the same productive capacities and/or they do not have the same choices of expected profit and risk. Thus, compared to wheat producers, producers of nuclear power plants accept a greater risk with the hope of a higher profit. Therefore can we really speak of a superprofit?

If, later on, wheat growers complain of having a profit lower than producers of nuclear power plants, they should recognise that they only had to decide to produce atomic power plants previously, this choice having always been open to them. As long as the freedom to produce exists, the concept of superprofit is totally meaningless. And the corresponding theories of atomistic competition and monopoly are also meaningless: They are based on criteria that do not bring any valuable information about the relevant economic processes; they lead, instead, to hiding the information and so to loss of knowledge. We can even say that the traditional distinction between pure and perfect competition and monopoly (or oligopoly) is not a scientific approach, since instead of explaining – which is the role of science – it merely provides a catalog based on arbitrary criteria. It is as if Newton, instead of explaining why an apple falls from the tree, had 'explained' that there are red apples and green apples and that the first ones are 'super-visible'. Can one understand phenomena if one restricts oneself to the observation of certain results at a given time (for instance, the existence of a large number or a small number of producers) without giving any attention to the processes that could bring about these results? The theories of atomistic competition and monopoly are *formally correct* – and this is why we will have the opportunity to use some elements of them – but the distinction made between the situation of competition and the situation of monopoly is based on a questionable criterion, that of the number of producers.

It is certainly understandable that a monopolist, if he or she has the opportunity, may decide to go to this point where the maximization of profit is made possible by the scarcity of the quantities supplied. But if there is a superprofit, why does nobody come to compete with him on this market? This should seem all the more likely that, according to the traditional theory of competition, profit is zero in the nonmonopolistic activities. Producers then have an interest in moving factors of production from these activities toward the monopolistic activities. In reality, everyone is trying to get superprofits by taking into account the specific information they have, their capacities, their targets.

Let us take an example which is simple but which may seem caricatured. An individual sees a coin on a sidewalk. He considers that the subjective cost in time and physical effort required to bend down and pick up the piece is lower than the value of this coin for him. He therefore makes a profit thanks to this activity of picking up the coin. It does not matter whether he went there by chance or because he had assumed that, this place being very busy, he could hope to find a coin. As a holder of a specific position or a specific knowledge he made a profit. Should we say that he got a superprofit, compared to a hypothetical situation in which all the individuals of the world would have had the same information, namely that a coin had fallen at this place? Should we say that this hypothetical situation would correspond to an optimum only to the extent that there are very large numbers of coin pickers and perfect information? Certainly not. However, it is a line of reasoning similar to that which is done in the theory of pure and perfect competition: one takes as a standard a hypothetical situation that has no real connection with the concrete conditions of human action.

Action is necessarily located in time, but the traditional theory of competition and monopoly is static. This is why it cannot give a correct account of producers' acts. Thus, the typical entrepreneur represented in the theory of atomistic competition has finally nothing of an entrepreneur except the name. Let us take the case of an individual who does not like risk, who enters as a producer into an already saturated market and who sells the same product as others at the same price (for instance, there are a million farmers and he takes from each one a millionth of his sales). He gets an income, but it is not of a very different nature from that of an employee. He is a sort of employee of himself. In a world where everything is almost certain, he promises to himself an income calculated from technically determined costs and from a sale price given by the market. In fact, this 'entrepreneur' is reduced to a role of organiser of work (as in a bureaucratic economy) and he has nothing of a true entrepreneur. He is therefore paid for his work exactly in the same way as any employee. He is also, possibly, paid for his contributions in capital. This remuneration is also certain and it therefore looks more like interest payment than a profit, as we have already seen.

Let us assume that there is a firm – among the very large number of firms in a given market – working thanks to the work of two people – among whom one would have the name of entrepreneur and the other the name of employee – and thanks to the loans of two creditors. Nothing would be changed by dividing this firm into two smaller firms, each with an 'entrepreneur' and a creditor. Under the assumption of perfect information, the employee and the 'entrepreneur' are interchangeable, because in reality the entrepreneurial function does not exist.

True entrepreneurs are totally different from the alleged entrepreneur of the theory of atomistic competition. They are in an uncertain environment – which means that information is not perfect – they innovate, they take risks. Their remuneration is residual, that is, it is equal to the difference between, on the one hand, the revenue obtained from the sales of products and, on the other hand, all of the money promised by contract with certainty (to employees, suppliers, lenders, owners of land and rented property, etc.). When they decide to enter a market, it is with a certain function of risk and a certain function of expected profit. We can therefore consider that the traditional theory of competition is not an economic theory, since it does not take account of the actual behaviour of those who act; it is a purely mechanical vision. It is, however, accepted as a standard by most economists and those who determine economic policy. This theory claims to reach a precise scientific conclusion, namely that the rate of profit becomes zero in a situation of pure and perfect competition. But what becomes zero should not be called a profit. Because the actual profit cannot exist in the universe assumed by this theory. As it is not incorporating the elements that explain the profit, it is normal that this theory leads to the idea that it is zero.

To better understand what is actually competition, we must go back to the basics of microeconomics. On Figure 4.1 we have represented different producers who have different supply curves. Therefore, it is assumed that at some point in time these different producers do not use the same techniques of production. The most efficient technique is that of the producer c and, assuming that perfect information will eventually prevail, all producers will converge to a situation identical to that of the producer c, in accordance with the principles of atomistic competition. For a given state of demand (D_1), three producers wish to produce, namely producers a, b, and c. Their cost curves being different, each one produces a different amount than others. The points they choose – namely A, B, and C for producers a, b, and c respectively – are such that they have no desire to produce more for the relative price level prevailing on the market. In accordance with the traditional

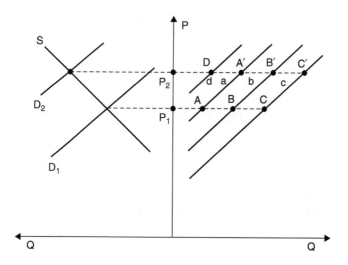

Figure 4.1

assumptions, the marginal profit of each producer is zero. But this statement necessarily gives rise to two series of remarks:

- First, when one says that the marginal profit is zero, one should indicate that it is the subjective profit. The statement that the producer equates the marginal cost and the marginal revenue actually means that he has no desire to produce more because, beyond the amount thus determined, the subjective costs outweigh the subjective expected profit. These gains and costs are not necessarily expressed in monetary terms. A baker may have the physical capacity to produce more loaves, but he would have to work many more hours and he prefers to arbitrate in favor of leisure and sleep. It is a matter of simple rationality to assume that an individual stops an activity as soon as he comes to prefer another one.

In other words, what is presented as a feature of competition in the traditional model (the existence of a zero marginal profit) is actually an absolutely general characteristic of human action. It means that an individual pursues an activity as long as it is more desirable for him or her than any other conceivable activity and he or she stops it when another activity becomes relatively more desirable. This implies that it is not possible to distinguish a situation of competition and a situation of monopoly using the fact that there would be no profit in the first case and a superprofit in the second one, because human behaviour is the same in both cases.

- On the other hand, saying that the marginal profit is zero does not mean that the total profit is zero. Indeed, all the units produced bring a profit to their producers, with the exclusion of the marginal unit that is precisely defined by the fact that, as regards it only, the profit becomes zero. The producer c, who is more efficient than the producers a and b, reaches a situation of zero marginal profit for a larger quantity of output. Producer c receives a total profit greater than them, since he produces the quantities produced by them at lower costs and since, moreover, he produces, in a cost-effective way, a larger quantity. Can we then say that the producer c makes a superprofit compared to the other producers? We see from this example that the superprofit can exist even with a large number of producers, provided that they are not identical. Certainly the producer c of our example makes a superprofit – or a higher profit – compared to an arbitrary standard according to which all producers would be exactly the same and would therefore get exactly the same profit. But should such a concept – namely the superprofit – be interesting and useful? We have seen that a rigorous evaluation of the theory of atomistic competition moved the mainspring of this theory to the assessment of the existence or nonexistence of a superprofit. What is important is not so much whether producers in a market are more numerous or fewer but their greater or lesser differentiation.

The traditional theory explains that the monopolist achieves a superprofit because he or she owns specific information, namely the knowledge of the reactions of the demanders. But it does not care about the ways by which this situation has occurred. However, what substantial difference may exist between this situation and the one we just saw – the one where there are many producers, but one of them has specific information, namely a knowledge of production techniques more efficient than others? What characterises the traditional theory of competition and monopoly is therefore not the number of producers on a market, contrary to what is usually stated, but some specific assumptions concerning the information held by producers. Thus, this theory calls 'competition' a situation in which producers are fully informed regarding their production techniques and perfectly ignorant regarding the behaviour of demanders on the market.

From a purely formal point of view one can possibly have fun developing the implications of a theory of this kind. But what becomes questionable is the claim that one can use it as an explanatory theory of the actual functioning of an economy or, *a fortiori*, the desire to give it the role of a normative theory. The arbitrary nature of this theory seems more obvious the more one refers to the actual behaviour of an entrepreneur. An entrepreneur is basically someone who watches the market, who tries to know the demand and the needs of customers. At the time when the entrepreneur has detected the possibility of opportunities for sales, he is therefore in a situation of relative informedness from the point of view of the market and of relative ignorance from the point of view of the techniques to be used to meet the needs of the market. The work will then be to find these techniques.

The use of the word 'profit' therefore leads to important ambiguities. The same term is used to refer to two totally different concepts. As we have already recalled, the profit should normally be defined as a residual income in a situation of uncertainty. It is a remuneration for those who take in charge the risks of production.

But the profit described by the traditional theory is a simple arithmetic difference between a price and a cost of production. In this case it would be more appropriate to speak of 'yield'. How is it expressed in the schematised example of Figure 4.1? Saying that there are different, more or less efficient production techniques means that they are not available perfectly and for free. The entrepreneur c, who has the most efficient technique, has therefore necessarily done a kind of bet: he has imagined the possibility of producing at lower costs, and has taken the risk of investing time and capital in research and development for the implementation of these techniques with the hope, precisely, to obtain a larger gain. If he had simply been content to copy the technique of the producer a, supposed to be available and known to all, he would have made a gain that we could call a yield (difference between a given price and given production costs without any uncertainty). But he has invested to obtain lower costs. The additional gain he got through this investment can precisely be called a profit; there is therefore no reason to speak of a superprofit. Can we not say exactly the same thing for the so-called superprofit of the monopolist?

Imagine indeed that demand increases (it shifts from D_1 to D_2 on Figure 4.1). The selling price goes from P_1 to P_2 and the producers a, b, and c move, respectively, to points A', B', and C' (where they equalise their marginal costs with the selling price). Producer d, who could not sell when demand was too low, can now enter the market, since the price has increased. Compared to d, producers a, b, and, above all, c seem to receive superprofits. But should we not say rather that they had anticipated the possibility of an expansion of demand, that they had arranged their production capacity accordingly, and that they thus receive the remuneration of a successful bet? If the demand, instead of increasing, had decreased, they would have made losses.

These different scenarios help to illustrate this idea that the concept of superprofit implies the prior determination of a 'normal' rate of profit and that it is necessarily decided arbitrarily. The concept of a superprofit is as nonexistent as that of a normal profit. This is obviously applicable to the case of a monopoly.

As is well known, as far as it is assumed that there is zero profit in one case (situation I, called 'pure and perfect competition') and superprofit in another (situation II, called 'monopoly'), one can deduce that the buyer is despoiled in situation II. But one must wonder about the reasons for this situation. Why is there no other producer in situation II, that is, a producer eager to enter into competition with the monopolist? Why does nobody have any interest in abandoning his or her current activity to come to the activity where positive profits are supposed to exist? But then why can we talk of a superprofit? Like any producer, the single producer stops production just before the (subjective) marginal profit can become negative.

If some apparent profit opportunities are not exploited, although everyone is free to come and to exploit them, this is necessarily because *nobody wants to do it*, for reasons that can be countless and which we probably do not know well. This may be because the risk is too large or because information costs are too high. Just as the notion of profit is subjective, the notion of superprofit is also necessarily subjective. Even if we do not know in detail these reasons, one can still say that, if someone does not enter an activity in which there is, in the opinion of an outside observer, a superprofit, this can be only for two broad categories of reasons:

- Either he or she considers that there is no superprofit *from his or her point of view*.
- Or else he or she is unable to enter this market.

In all cases, therefore, it is not the number of producers in a market that determines the profit or the superprofit. The only important consideration concerns the possibility of entering a market. This is why we will propose *to define competition as the situation in which there is freedom to enter a market*. It is striking to note that this definition is perfectly in agreement with what is meant in ordinary language when talking about competition. When one says that a producer has to face the competition of another producer, one does not care about knowing whether there is a large number of producers. What matters is whether there is a possibility to come into a market to compete with those who are already in this market.

If there is only one producer – a monopolist, according to the traditional theory – in a given market at a given time, if there is freedom to enter this market and if no one does, it is a proof that there is no superprofit nor, of course, any despoilment of buyers. If no one takes the opportunity to enjoy what could be called a freedom to despoil others, it is because the despoilment is purely fictitious. *The theory of monopoly is formally correct, but it is applied in an incorrect way.*

Let us consider again Figure 3.2 in which – let us remember – we have assumed, to simplify the representation, that the marginal cost, C_m, was constant, regardless of the scale of production (so that the average cost is equal and is also constant). The point T is supposed to be the point of pure and perfect competition (intersection of the curve of average revenue – or demand curve – and of the marginal cost curve), while the two points R and S are supposed to represent the position of the monopoly, the superprofit being equal to RS (sale at a price P_2 greater than the marginal cost C_2). Two interpretations of this figure may be given, in addition to what we already know:

- Either the curve C_m is the true marginal cost curve and one can wonder why nobody exploits the potential gains that exist by going to point T, if there is freedom of entry into the market.
- Or the true marginal cost curve is C_{mc}, for example because there are increasing costs to discover and to exploit markets or risk costs, and then the point T has no meaning, there is no superprofit and it does not matter whether there are several producers on the market or a single one (threatened by the potential competition of new entrants). T then represents a purely dreamed point and it is therefore nonoperational. One cannot compare an existing situation to an inconceivable situation that is arbitrarily considered as optimal. As Gerald O'Driscoll has stressed, all costs required to bring a good in a usable form to the final consumer have an equal status. These costs can be, for instance, information costs, marketing costs, sale costs, risk costs, which can be rightly considered as increasing with the scale of production. One

begins by exploiting the most accessible portions of the market, and then one explores portions that are more and more difficult to access and which are increasingly uncertain. These costs have obviously nothing to do with the number of producers.

Succeeding in making production scarcer – it is undeniable – permits making an extra profit. But to be able to create scarcity, it is not enough to be the only producer of a good; it is necessary to find the means to maintain such a scarcity, that is, to prevent others from entering the market.

Going back to price discrimination

Let us refer again to Figure 3.2. We have seen previously that the curve representing C_{mc} – the 'true' marginal cost curve – has an upward-growing slope, which can be explained, for instance, by the existence of costs to discover and to develop markets, as well as risk costs. But it can also be explained by the existence of costs of exclusion or discrimination, as we have seen in Chapter 3, if the monopolist producer is able to do price discrimination. And there is certainly no doubt that, in this case, only a monopoly or a cartel would have the opportunity to practise discrimination. One could then be tempted to say that a nonmonopoly situation is preferable, since it makes discrimination impossible and since, as a result, consumers benefit from lower prices.

However, one should look at the problem otherwise, and refrain from condemning the monopoly under the pretext that it makes discrimination possible. One should indeed wonder why there is only one producer in the considered market. However, two explanations are possible[1]:

- There is only one producer because other producers are prevented from entering this market. What is relevant is not the fact that there is only one producer, but the fact that there is no freedom to enter into the market.
- Freedom to enter is perfect, but there is only one producer who, moreover, practises price discrimination, because, in the absence of this policy of price discrimination, the activity in question would not be profitable enough, compared to other opportunities, to justify the entry of a producer on this market. And since buyers prefer to buy the good in question, despite price discrimination, rather than to buy another good, it is obviously because the situation in which the good is sold with discrimination is perceived by them as superior to the situation where it would not be sold at all. One cannot say that there is superprofit and despoilment of consumers. In fact, if one claimed that the consumer is despoiled, this statement would be made by reference to a situation *which cannot exist*, taking into account the specific characteristics of the concerned market. Indeed, if the entry into the market is free and nobody takes advantage of this freedom, it is because the activity in question is not attractive if price discrimination is not possible. However, we have seen that the increase in the number of producers makes it more and more difficult to do price discrimination, since it implies necessarily a cartel agreement.

If discrimination was prohibited, it could occur that the good in question would not be produced because it would not be profitable enough (compared to other activities) and the satisfaction of consumers would suffer.

Let us place ourselves at a moment of time where several potential producers are considering various possibilities of production and let us assume that price discrimination is not possible in activities A and B, but that it is possible in activity C. Assuming that the risk is the same everywhere, to have the same rate of profit in all three activities, it may happen that it is necessary to make a discrimination policy in activity C, which only a monopolist can do. But it may be that, in addition, there is only one producer in A and many producers in B. What can explain this particular structure of production at one given time? The existence of only one producer in the activity C may be the result of specific characteristics of this activity that are such that it is profitable only in the case of price discrimination and that discrimination, precisely, is possible. But the existence of only one producer in the activity A is explained by totally different reasons. It may be the result of chance, but more likely the result of different firm strategies, of different assessments of risk, of a differentiation of information. If entry is free in all markets, it is likely that the monopoly situation will disappear in the activity A, but not in the activity C, at least as long as the technological evolution has not made this activity profitable in the absence of discrimination.

The consequences of free competition

As opposed to pure and perfect competition – or atomistic competition – let us call 'free competition' the situation where there is freedom to enter a market, which means, in fact, entrepreneurial freedom. As we have seen, in the case of pure and perfect competition, the entrepreneur is attempting to comply with a reference model: Producing an homogenous good, he or she adopts *the* technique of production considered as technically optimal and adopted by other producers. It is, therefore, the *homogeneity* of products and producers which defines atomistic competition. Free competition is defined from the process that characterises the market: there is competition when there is free entry on the market, regardless of the consequences resulting therefrom. It may occur that competition, thus defined, leads to the coexistence of a large number of nearly identical producers producing a homogenous good (which would be more or less the case, for example, for producers of wheat in the world). But in reality it does not matter whether there is a small or a large number of producers or even a single producer, *at a given point of time*, on a market. And competition will prevail as well, even if, at some point, there is only one producer, provided that there is freedom to enter the market.

Many reasons may exist to explain why it may happen that only one producer is present on a market at a given time, while there is free entry, that is, competition. This may be the case because the produced good is particularly indivisible and a multiplicity of producers is not really conceivable (space rockets, aircraft carriers, etc.). But we also met the case in which only price discrimination could allow a profitable production, which implied the existence of a single producer or, at least, of a cartel: a restricted number of producers coordinating their decisions to produce as if there was a single producer.

But more generally, we can say that *the great merit of free competition is that it leads to 'monopolistic' situations, that is, to the existence of a single producer.* This may seem paradoxical. Yet such a proposal is the only one to be consistent with a realistic theory of the entrepreneur. As we have seen, the one who truly deserves the name of entrepreneur is not this kind of 'robot' of the pure and perfect competition model, but the one who innovates and who receives a profit as an award for his or her innovative capacities and ability to take risks. Now, the one who innovates is the one who supplies a new good before others, or who, at least, changes the processes of production in such a way that he or she is the only one able to supply an existing good at a lower price. Far from conforming to an unchanging model, the entrepreneur offers a different product or a cheaper product. If there is free entry into markets, entrepreneurs are encouraged to enter actually, in order to compete with existing producers, not to do like them, but, on the contrary, to do *better than they do.*

Any innovator is necessarily alone on a market, the market that is defined by the new product. From the point of view of the traditional theory, he or she is a monopolist, since the market share is equal to 100 percent for the product in question. And because the entrepreneur is the only producer on that market, one says that he or she receives a superprofit compared to a situation of pure and perfect competition. But this situation of pure and perfect competition, used as a standard in the traditional theory, is purely mythical, since, until the arrival of the innovator, no producer had imagined producing this new good. It is therefore ridiculous to say that there must be a very large number of producers producing a homogenous good for competition to prevail. By postulating the existence of a large number of producers and a homogenous good, the atomistic theory of competition therefore leads to absurdities.

By blindly applying the traditional theory, one must say that the innovative entrepreneur who launches a new product and who, at least for a while, is alone on that market, receives a superprofit, meaning that he or she despoils consumers in comparison with a situation of pure and perfect competition. However, it is not a superprofit but purely and simply a profit: the residual remuneration received by an entrepreneur. At the time when an entrepreneur decides the production of a new good, because there is freedom to enter markets, he or she takes risks – losing capital and wasting time for nothing – but the innovator does it because he hopes to get a profit which is satisfactory. It is this potential 'monopoly profit', which is actually an 'innovation profit', which gives the entrepreneur the incentive to act, which is the engine of action and the factor of economic progress. Because it is purely residual, it is never certain and its exact value is unknown in advance.

According to the traditional theory, the higher this profit – this superprofit – the greater is the despoilment of consumers. Now, there could be despoilment, that is, robbery, only if all of the gain of exchange could be confiscated or even more, if some of the traders could be totally deprived of their share of the earnings from exchange. In this case, moreover, there could not be any more exchange. In reality, the profit's importance rises as the exchange gains rise, which means that the entrepreneur better meets the needs of buyers. Far from despoiling them, the entrepreneur increases their well-being. The gains due to innovation are shared between the producer – who receives a profit – and the buyers, who benefit from products and services that are better for them and/or less expensive. Production costs are not, indeed, *data* of a technical nature. New products or new methods of production to lower costs can only be discovered under the pressure of competition. As Friedrich Hayek has often written, *competition is a process of discovery*.

On Figure 4.2 we have represented the demand curve or curve of average revenue for a given good, R_A. Let us assume initially that we are in a situation of atomistic competition, represented by the curves C_m and C_A resulting from the aggregation of the individual curves of all firms in this sector of production. It is assumed that all these firms are identical and that the point of longterm equilibrium is point A (where the marginal cost curve and the average revenue curve go through the minimum of the average cost curve, as it has been shown in Figure 2.3, and where profit is zero). The price charged to the consumer is P_1. Let us imagine now that an innovative entrepreneur arrives on this market. His marginal cost curve and his average cost curve, C_{mi} and C_{Ai}, are located under those of his competitors of the atomistic competition situation. It is optimal for him to sell a quantity Q_2 at a price P_2, since this quantity corresponds to the equalization of the marginal revenue and the marginal cost. His unit profit is equal to RS, that is, the difference between the average revenue and the average cost. According to the traditional theory, this 'monopolist' would make a superprofit in comparison with the situation of pure and perfect competition, which would imply that producers be at point T where profits are zero. But this point does not correspond to any reality, since, precisely,

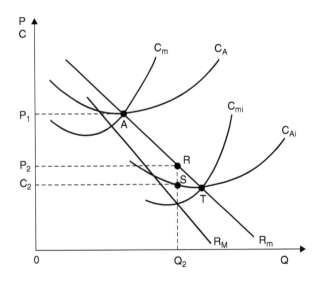

Figure 4.2

production by a very large number of producers can be done only at point A. When, on this market, one moves from a situation with a very large number of producers (pure and perfect competition) to a situation with a single producer (monopoly), there is a gain for buyers, since the price declines, and there is not a despoilment, as claimed by the traditional theory.

But it is clear that one is not going to remain indefinitely at the same position. First, since entering the market is free, the innovator will be followed by imitators who have seen a possibility of profit. By increasing the amount of goods supplied, they move the market equilibrium point to point T, and of course, the profit of the innovator will decrease gradually. This means that the profit of the monopolist can be temporary, insofar as there is free entry into the market. In addition, innovation may well continue in this sector. It may be done by the first innovator or another producer. There is then a continuous cycle of innovation profits, gradually curtailed by the imitators and followed by new profits from innovation. Economic progress, in a situation of free competition, therefore translates into successive periods in which producers make efforts for the differentiation of products, possibly followed by periods of homogenization of products. The theory of pure and perfect competition, with its rigid and static assumptions of homogeneity of goods and multiplicity of producers, is so far unable to account for real economic life.

Strangely enough, competition in economic activities has more to do with the other competitive activities of life than with the theoretical conceptualization of economic competition provided by economists. Indeed, when talking about competition between people – whether athletes or students – one means precisely an effort to *differentiate* – to find a unique and better position – and certainly not a search for homogeneous results. The atomistic theory of competition, which is formally correct, is based on concepts that are wrong. It is therefore not usable and it is regrettable that it is so widely accepted and used.

Note

1 We will see a third, much more important explanation in the next section when taking a dynamic view of competition.

5 True and false breaches of competition

The atomistic theory of competition is a pure intellectual construction that does not allow one to understand competition in the real world. One may therefore wonder why it remains the dominant theory. The reason is probably the assimilation that is made between a situation of pure and perfect competition and economic optimum. But this optimum is itself defined in a questionable way, since it is purely static and technical and since it does not allow one to understand the nature and the role of profit and innovation. Yet, it is this atomistic theory that inspires all policies that are supposed to protect competition.

The traditional theory of monopoly, meanwhile, has been built as a counterpoint to the theory of pure and perfect competition: The idea according to which a monopoly brings a superprofit is perfectly consistent with the idea that competition leads to an economic optimum: a situation in which no one is despoiled and in which productive capacities are used at their maximum. In fact, this traditional theory of monopoly is not strictly wrong; it is its use which is wrong. It should not apply to a situation in which the conditions of pure and perfect competition are not carried out; it should apply only to a situation where there is a lack of freedom to enter a market.

Public violations of free competition

The traditional theory has an obsession with what is called a 'monopoly power' and the pure and perfect competition model is constructed in such a way that nobody has such power over others. But this theory actually obscures completely the real phenomena of power, and it is based on a serious conceptual confusion. The concerned power, indeed, is not a power of coercion. If free entry prevails on a market and only one producer is present, one obviously cannot say that he got this position by coercion, since, by definition, entry is free. It is indeed contradictory to say that both freedom and coercion obtain. And if ever this producer is alone in a market because he or she has used coercion, the real problem is not that he or she is the only producer, but that the producer has gotten this position by using coercion. In other words, as Friedrich Hayek has so often pointed out, one cannot evaluate a phenomenon from the simple observation of the result (for example, the fact of being a single producer), but from the process that led to this result. It makes a considerable difference whether a position has been reached through coercion, or by the mere exercise of one's own talents (as we have seen in the case of an innovator). In the first case there is a phenomenon of power which does not obtain in the second.

Let us take the case of the 'monopoly' which we studied in Chapter 4, that is, this situation of temporary monopoly resulting from innovation. It certainly follows that the producer receives better information than if there were large numbers of producers, in the sense that such a producer can better forecast the reactions of demand to changes in the quantities supplied (as stated by the traditional theory of monopoly). But this particular information is not the result of a privilege obtained by force; it results only from a particular effort intended precisely to put oneself in such a situation, which all other producers were also free to do. And we have also seen that the possibility of being temporarily the single producer of a good was a key driver of human action.

Competition policy

Because this asymmetry of situation between a single (innovative) producer and other producers is often (wrongly) viewed as an asymmetry of power, one creates supposed 'checks and balances' in order to re-establish equality between producers. This is the origin of 'competition policies' which are implemented by most states or international organizations (for instance the European Union). These interventions are based on the underlying idea that a certain equality of position is needed to have a fair economic system. One then arrives at an extraordinary paradox: one uses the power of coercion of states to break an asymmetry of power that is actually nonexistent. In other words, if the freedom to act led to the existence of a single producer in some specific markets, one will introduce coercion in the functioning of these markets although it was totally absent. And as the state is benefiting from the monopoly of legal coercion, one therefore introduces in markets an asymmetry in the power of coercion.

Thus, *all the laws that are supposed to protect competition in fact destroy it* and this is why one must store them in the catalogue of true infringements of competition. More specifically, because these laws claim to defend something which is actually nonexistent – pure and perfect competition – they tend to destroy real, free competition. Indeed, they usually take as a criterion of noncompetitive situations the market shares of firms. We have already seen previously that the definition of a market is necessarily arbitrary, because it depends on the more or less precise definition of goods. But what is obviously the most questionable position is to consider that competition exists – and is desirable – when each firm present on a market has only a very small market share. Of course, the underlying rationale for this procedure is to remove the so-called superprofits by preventing a firm from having a 'dominant position' on a market. It is claimed that one can thus oblige a monopoly – or an oligopoly – to operate *as if* pure and perfect competition existed. However, we know that this claim is absolutely unjustified, since it is impossible to know what would happen if pure and perfect competition existed. It thus follows from these laws that one confiscates by coercion a supposed superprofit that has not been obtained by coercion. Although arbitrary, the atomistic theory of competition is widely adopted and it serves as a reference theory to assess concrete situations. Because it is a normative theory, and because reality is not consistent with the theoretical model, one will then attempt to force reality to fit the theory. This is the basis of competition policies.

To fight against 'monopoly power', as defined by the traditional theory, the state has a large range of means. For example, it can require a firm to be split into several pieces or to abandon an activity in which it has a 'too large market share'. It may issue regulations to prevent producers from developing some of their activities, it may force them to sell at lower prices, which are claimed to correspond to the prices of pure and perfect competition (although these prices are nonexistent and therefore unknown). It may nationalise firms under the pretext of refunding to consumers and citizens the superprofits of monopolies. It may forbid a firm to hold the equity capital of a subsidiary beyond some arbitrarily fixed percentage, it may forbid two or more firms to merge, and so on.

Given the previous statements we have made, it is clear that these measures are harmful, since they prevent firms from reaching their optimal size or from deciding their strategies freely. Thus they are also harmful for potential buyers, since the efficiency of enterprises and their innovative capacities are thus reduced. They also increase the risk of entrepreneurial activity. Indeed, an entrepreneur who has introduced an important innovation and who hoped to get a satisfactory return by keeping a 'monopoly' position for some time knows that he risks being stopped by a competition policy which is necessarily arbitrary and therefore unpredictable.

When one says that a firm 'controls' such or such percentage of a market, one is confusing two different things. A firm controls its resources, because it owns them, but it does not control the market, except if it has means to exert coercion. As Thomas Sowell writes, 'historically, market shares have changed over time – some drastically – and in some cases the so-called dominant firm has disappeared entirely. *Life* magazine and the Graflex Corporation are recent examples. Once the Graflex Corporation sold virtually all the cameras used by newspaper photographers. But they 'controlled' nothing; there were always many other domestic and foreign producers of press cameras, and almost all of them disappeared along with Graflex when improvements in smaller-sized cameras made the latter effective substitutes'.[1]

Public coercion

The only case where there is a true breach to competition is the one where freedom of entry is made impossible. However, this may correspond to two different situations:

- There is a private coercion exerted by producers installed on a market to prevent the entry of newcomers. Because they undermine the legitimate rights of others these acts are obviously reprehensible. But the possible judicial punishment is specifically related to this causal coercive factor and not to the fact that there is, at one given time, a small number of producers in a market. From this point of view it is therefore not necessary to elaborate a specific competition law.

- There is a public coercion that prevents the free entry on the market. It is the case, for example, when laws or regulations prohibit the production of a good by others than those who are expressly authorised. This is the case, of course, of all public monopolies. Thus, in many countries, one cannot freely enter the air transport market, only the national central bank has the right to issue banknotes, a public firm has a monopoly on rail transportation of people or in the distribution of mail, etc. The consequences of these monopoly situations, resulting from the exercise of public coercion, are the same whether the firms that receive State privileges are public or private.

One of the ways by which public authorities restrict the entry into a market is protectionism. Now, it is a paradox of modern politics that the state can, on the one hand, impose legislation allegedly in favour of competition – although it is not necessary and it may even have anticompetitive effects – and that, on the other hand, it is the only real source of monopoly power. There is in fact a fundamental difference between a monopoly of public origin and the situation described above where a firm happens to be the sole producer in a market. In the first case, competition – defined as freedom of entry into a market – is definitely excluded, by definition, while in the second case it exists and we have even seen that it may precisely explain the existence of only one producer in a given market. Yet, strangely enough, any legislation in favour of competition applies to so-called private monopolies (defined by the size of their market share) and it applies generally not to the monopolies of public origin, that is, the only ones that deserve really this name, since they correspond effectively to a ban on any entry into the market for other than the monopolist *or*, at least, for others than the small number of producers who are eligible to participate in a cartel of public origin.[2] Similarly, public authorities tackle situations in which freedom of entry does exist and they decline to accept global free trade, which would constitute the best competition policy. In fact, experience proves that, in an economy protected from international competition, producers have much less incentive to innovate because the impulse given to the 'discovery process' is much lightened.

We have previously stressed that the monopoly theory was formally correct, but that it was not applied correctly since the idea of a superprofit is meaningless when there is freedom of entry into a market. However, it is perfectly valid when this freedom does not exist. The producer who is thus placed in a monopoly position, thanks to the use of public coercion, can make sold quantities scarcer and thus obtain a superprofit.[3] Thus, one can analyze a protectionist policy as the exercise of a monopoly power: the inhabitants of a country must pay a higher price for goods that are available in smaller quantities.[4] Similarly, the monopoly of the central bank for the production of banknotes, reinforced by legal tender laws – requiring residents of a country to use only the national currency – and possibly by exchange controls, leads to a scarcity of *real* cash-balances and a higher cost of money, in the form of an 'inflation tax'.[5]

State activity also provides a good example of discriminating monopoly. It can indeed be considered that the state is a monopoly producer of what may be called 'public goods', namely the set of goods corresponding to public spending. Now, the price that is asked for the provision of this composite good is tax. But this tax is not the same according to the concerned 'customers'. Thus the progressive tax is precisely characterised by the fact that the state imposes a different price according to the users of state services.

We have seen that competition faced an unavoidable obstacle when entering into a market is made impossible by public coercion. But, one may say, it may also be restricted for other reasons that do not involve any public intervention. The traditional argument in this sense is to say that in many cases the existing producer enjoys a 'privilege' over potential entrants, because he is already present on the market, he knows this market, he can avoid some expenditures to promote his products, he has written off a large part of the initial installation costs, etc.[6] But this argument is not an economic or even a moral argument. It is an argument that arbitrarily considers as a valuable criterion the fact that everyone is in the same situation, and which therefore erases the historical dimension of human activity. It induces a wrong notion of equality and distributive morality, as if one could make all individuals perfectly identical. However, how could one put a producer on trial for having been present in a market before others, even though there was freedom to enter when he started his activity? Such a producer has therefore only taken risks that others have not dared to take, or has looked for particularly valid information on a potential market or on a particular production process.

Generally freedom is defined negatively, as the absence of coercion. Thus, freedom of entry into a market is defined as the absence of coercion to produce and to supply the fruits of one's production. The deep reason why the above argument is unacceptable is therefore the following: Saying that a particular producer has distinct advantages over others does not mean that entry into a market is not free, if these advantages have not been obtained by coercion but only by the free activity of the beneficiary and his specific capabilities. *What is objectionable is privilege, but not superiority.* Another kind of argument uses the same abusive extension in the meaning of words, by implicitly assuming that any inequality in situations corresponds to an unjustifiable privilege. Such is the case with the theory of the natural monopoly, which we now consider.

Natural monopolies and cartels

There are in various activities certain specific situations in which the cost of a particular production is lower when it is made by a single firm rather than by several firms that would have to share the market. It is for instance the case when there are indivisibilities or economies of scale, so that the unit costs for a product are lower for larger firms. But it can also be the case where complementarities between different productions make it possible to save resources. One therefore says in such cases that there are *natural monopolies*.

In the context of the traditional theory the following dilemma arises: it is technically optimal to have a single firm in the concerned activity, but, not having to face any competitor, there is a risk that this firm is asking too high a price and that it despoils buyers by taking advantage of its monopoly position. One usually draws the consequence that the state must intervene to avoid this risk of despoilment by nationalizing the concerned firm or by regulating it to prevent it from asking unjustifiably high prices. A public producer would likely impose prices closer to production costs, thus avoiding the 'monopoly superprofit'. One would then have the benefits of competition, without the disadvantages potentially caused by the existence of decreasing costs.

But what could be the viewpoint of the theory of free competition? Freedom of entry into the market is in principle guaranteed, but it can appear as a purely formal freedom, since no firm has an interest to come and to compete with a firm that is already present on the market and which can, for instance, produce at an optimal production scale. Any newcomer, indeed, is confronted with the risk of not being able to produce otherwise than at a suboptimal level.

But decisions cannot be based solely on technical considerations. Only economic considerations may determine the procedures by which both costs and needs can be revealed and therefore determine the optimal level of production. Now, it can be shown that these types of problems can be solved in a system of freedom. If there is a possibility of profit thanks to the 'coordination' of different producers or of some of their activities – for example, to achieve a certain scale of production – the firm that is subject to a current or potential competition is best suited to seek these opportunities of profit and to benefit from them.

In fact, first of all, competition is characterised not only by the freedom of choice of consumers and producers, but by the free functioning of the financial market. Let us assume that, for certain activities, a single producer is needed for some technological reasons. It remains no less true that management and investment choices must be made, and they can be considered as optimal only by reference to a market. Choices to be made are not only technical choices, they are economic choices. A public monopoly does not ensure the best possible working of this control system because it is convinced that it will remain on its market, regardless of the quality of its management, due to the lack of free competition.

Conversely, suppose that we have a system of private property rights and that, for certain activities in an area, there is, at a given time, only one producer. This does not mean that competition is necessarily absent, implying, in the opinion of some, the need for nationalization or a regulation (to mimic competition so as to prevent the despoilment of the consumer). First, a new competitor may appear, if there is freedom of entry into the market. One can imagine that though a single producer was present on the market in the past, now that conditions have changed there is room for another producer. On the other hand, if there is freedom of entry into the market, there are incentives to adopt new technologies, which may well threaten the apparent monopoly positions (for example, cable television came to compete with traditional hertzian TV networks).

But let us imagine that the existence of a single producer can be explained by sustainable causes. The fact remains that financial markets imply the existence of a fundamental adjustment mechanism, namely the transfer of property rights. It can be done thanks to bankruptcy, if the single producer is particularly inefficient, so that its production will be taken over by a more efficient producer. But the mechanism of the takeover bid avoids such a solution in many cases and it allows selection of the most efficient producers. This is obviously not possible when production is carried out by a public institution or a private firm that enjoys a public privilege for doing business.[7]

One may also say that the free working of competition may create the risk that the facilities of a producer become obsolete before they can be written off, because of the emergence of another producer who will put in place new structures of production to satisfy a clientele already served by the first producer. There would be a 'social waste' due to the fact that these externalities among producers are not taken into account. It is frequently believed that a monopoly – either public or private – would prevent such a waste. But this argument, if it was valid, would be valid for all productions and not only for those we are considering, that is, those where technological constraints impose a limited number of producers or even a single producer. This risk always exists, for a shopkeeper located on a street who suddenly sees a new competitor, as well as for an aircraft manufacturer. But it only means that one is never fully informed about the future. The producer who benefited from what seemed to be a natural monopoly believed in the existence of this monopoly, due to the existing and predictable state of techniques. At the moment a technique changes unexpectedly, the optimum production process is no longer the same. This is why, of course, producers are always trying to get the support of public power to restrict access to their own market and they always find arguments for this. But, as regards consumers, they would always benefit from a situation in which free access is preserved.

Let us admit therefore, as we have done so far, that there are technical reasons to explain that, at a given time, only a small number of producers are present in a market.[8] The general problem to be solved is the following: Which are the market structures that may reconcile two seemingly irreconcilable requirements: minimizing the waste due to the phenomena mentioned above; and maintaining competition, that is, freedom of entry into markets?

It is generally admitted that one can identify this type of situation *a priori* and from purely technical data, and that one must then necessarily choose between the benefits of the 'monopolisation' of an activity and the supposed benefits of competition. However, one should not mix up the fact that there is a single product, at one given time, in one given area, with the fact that there is only one producer. Structures of coordination between producers can be imagined without limits and it is precisely the role of the market to imagine them: saying that there is need for homogenisation of a product does not mean necessarily that there must be a single producer and, even less, that this producer must be public. 'Cartelisation' of production is the answer to the problem. This strategy reconciles the need for 'homogenisation' of the product (the opposite of what is normally caused by free competition, namely the diversification of products), while preserving at least some of the benefits of competition, which we have defined as the freedom of entry into a market.

The very general answer which we propose is therefore as follows: in cases of this kind, the optimal market structure is to combine cartel or monopoly structures within a system with competition outside this system. To arrange an activity according to a monopolistic market structure on the side of supply one can proceed in three different ways:

- A very big firm is the single producer of the good for which there are, for instance, economies of scale. It does not matter much, at the limit, whether it is a public or a private-regulated firm (enjoying exclusive rights on the market). A nearby case is that where the large firm coexists with small satellites, more or less dependent on it (for example, subcontractors).

- Several firms coordinate their production (their prices, their standards, etc.). There is homogenisation of the product, but there are different 'profit centers'. Stimulation among these different centers can thus be hoped for. A risk – but perhaps also, as we shall see, an advantage – can come from the behaviour of a *free rider*, meaning that a producer is not respectful of the rules of the game and tries to increase its market share. The common benefit is maximised by homogenisation and the coordination of production. The sharing of the market, which is implied by the existence of a cartel, can be such, for instance in the field of telecommunications, that in a cabling system one of the members of the cartel supplies the 'highway' (the cable) and other producers provide switching systems and/or local area networks, rather than each trying to have a communication highway. The roles of each producer can also be redistributed if a new highway is necessary. From this point of view, the structure with multiple decision-making centers is preferable to the existence of a single producer, since there is thus mutual stimulation. But as long as only a sole highway is necessary, it would be inefficient for a firm that was supposed to implement a specific task, (for instance the construction of a local network) to embark on the construction of a such a highway. The cartel is meant to allow producers to achieve gains where they are possible. It is therefore optimal that there is discipline in the cartel (due to the decreasing costs), which is not always easy to get, but the cartel is probably preferable to monopoly, because it allows a better set of incentives.

Thus we find here the usual characteristics of a cartel: by coordinating and offering an homogeneous product (possibly a complex one), the members of the cartel are able to exploit a monopoly position with the benefits and the risks that it implies. These benefits and risks include: specific advantages in the cases (and only in the cases) in which there are opportunities to gain by the coordination of production decisions; general risks because of the possible existence of a 'monopoly superprofit'. The organizational problem consists in making possible the centralization or the coordination gains while minimizing the risk of monopolisation and despoilment of the consumer. However, there are two ways to minimise these risks:

- The first way is related to the internal structure of the system. It is preferable that the monopoly position be operated by a cartel rather than by a single firm. In fact, the existence of several independent producers within a cartel makes it more difficult to exploit the monopoly situation and it is in this sense that we could say, above, that the behaviour of free riding was fortunate for the cartel (or, more precisely, for the customers of the cartel). In fact, any cartel is unstable because there are two conflicting forces. All participants have an interest in the exploitation of the monopoly situation, but each has an interest in increasing its own share of the common market and therefore to differentiate, in one way or another, from its partners. If 'coordination' gains are important, a member of the cartel is less tempted to leave the cartel (it would be difficult for this producer to offer a competitive price by leaving the cartel). In this case, the monopoly superprofit represents the confiscation by the cartel of a portion of the coordination gain. But the annual gain due to coordination by the cartel is shared: a share goes to the cartel and a share goes to consumers. The cartel is limited, in its possible attempt to confiscate the whole coordination gain, by the fear that free riding behaviours appear (namely the ability to offer competitive prices and to increase one's market share, that is, to compensate lower prices by greater sales). The monopolist is not restricted by this fear.

Furthermore, it may happen that the gains due to the coordination of production decisions change, because of the evolution of techniques. For instance, let us imagine a situation where these gains have a decreasing importance in the provision of a particular service. When the cost of coordination in the cartel (for instance, the acceptance of restrictions on the expansion of market shares) becomes too high compared with the gains due to coordination, there is free riding; once more, the market (the coexistence of decision-making centers that are, at least potentially, independent) makes it possible to solve with great flexibility the problems related to the gains due to the homogenisation of production, by facilitating the identification of these situations and their evolution.

• The second way to restrict the despoilment of consumers by a system of monopolisation and cartelisation is obviously to allow external competition. One can thus avoid having all or almost all of the coordination gains confiscated by the cartel or the monopoly; also avoided would be a monopoly superprofit higher than coordination gains, so that consumers lose in comparison with a situation of competition. Usual approaches implicitly assume that this is always the case, and that public monopolies or private-regulated monopolies make it possible to get the coordination gains and to refund them at least in part to consumers by acting 'as if' competition existed. We believe that it is neither necessary nor desirable to do 'as if', and that *actual* competition is the best solution. There is a sharing of the potential coordination gains between producers and consumers due to external competition, the freedom of entry of new producers on the market. This potential entry makes it impossible to exploit a monopoly profit beyond coordination gains. From this point of view, it is strange that, so often, states can both create public monopolies, especially in what they call 'public services', on the pretext of preventing the monopolist despoilment of consumers, and prevent competition from foreign producers of these same goods and services.

Consumers, in fact, naturally prefer producers who offer them a portion of the coordination gain and producers will be encouraged to enter a market if they can keep a share of this same gain. But one cannot decide *a priori* and as an external observer the 'optimal' distribution of coordination gains. It depends on the concrete preferences of each and the other. It is certain that the consumer is not protected by the existence of an internal monopoly structure, but by *the existence of external competition*. The usual reasoning does not distinguish between these two characteristics of market structures, and the concept of monopoly that is used in general is debatable. The fact that a monopoly (or cartel) structure may exploit a coordination gain does not imply meanwhile that there is a possibility of obtaining a monopoly profit, if external competition exists – that is, if the freedom to enter a market exists.

In other words, a system can be arranged in four different ways:

- Internal competition without external competition, which means that there is a protected market.
- Internal cartel or monopoly (public or private-regulated) and no external competition.
- Internal cartelisation and external competition (competition of potential entrants or competition from substitute products).
- Internal and external competition.

In cases where a cartel structure is justified for technical reasons, its efficiency (or its harmlessness from the point of view of the possible existence of a monopoly profit) is all the greater when there is more external competition. That is to say, once more, that competition is desirable, but that it must be defined, purely and simply, as the freedom to enter a market.

Notes

1 Sowell (1980), p. 205.
2 The term *monopoly* originally designated in England a royal privilege. It is the corporation of economists who gave it later the inappropriate meaning we have seen previously.
3 This superprofit is not always clearly visible because it can be "internalised", which means that it is retrieved by the employees in the form of various benefits, reduced working time, overstaffing or wastes.
4 One can refer to Chapter 8 of the present book for more concerning this statement.
5 One may refer to our book, Salin (2016).
6 A similar argument is often made in order to justify the protection of new economic activities (it is the so-called 'infant-industry argument'). In fact, this argument is not acceptable, as we explain in Chapter 10 of the present book.
7 This is the case, for instance, in some countries in which radio and TV frequencies are assigned to private firms and associations by a 'regulatory' body, so that there is no competition.
8 This seems to be particularly the case in network activities, that is, communication and telecommunication systems or in the field of money production.

6   How far competition?

A considerable expansion can be given to the word 'competition'. Indeed, it is in the very nature of human beings to compete, because goods are scarce and all are competing for the use of these goods, but also because all are different one from the other, and they try to differentiate, particularly to be better than others. That is why, in a sense, competition cannot be suppressed. But it may obey different rules. Access to scarce goods may come from coercion, whether physical or legal: in the latter case some of the competitors get what they want thanks to an allocation of legal privileges (what we have called a monopoly). Adam Smith had already pointed out that competition is beneficial when it corresponds to 'laws of justice': when 'Every man, as long as he does not violate the laws of justice, is left perfectly free to pursue his own interest his own way, and to bring both his industry and capital into competition with those of any other man, or order of men'.[1] This is the reason we have focused on what we called 'free competition' rather than on the traditional model of pure and perfect competition.

It is also why 'competition' should be defined as freedom to enter a market. Now, a market can be defined as this (abstract) place on which people are trading. Therefore, we can say that competition implies freedom for two partners to enter into a relationship of exchange. Everyone is free to propose services or goods, everyone is free to accept or to decline an exchange. Free competition is therefore similar to freedom of contract. Speaking about competition is speaking about freedom of contract. Are there natural limits to the exercise of this freedom of contract? In the opposite direction, would it be desirable to extend the concept of competition beyond the realm that traditionally appears to be the one of so-called competitive activities? This is the double question we now address.

The limits of contractual freedom

Previously we reviewed the argument, concerning 'natural monopoly', that free competition may lead to a waste of resources, so that it would be appropriate to impose limits. In fact, even in the case of so-called natural monopoly, free entry on the market is the optimal institutional arrangement. But another type of argument leads also to the idea that limits be brought to free competition. It is the case with the traditional theory of public goods and the more general theory of externalities.

Traditionally one defines a public good as a good with two characteristics: non-exclusivity and nonrivalry. Nonexclusivity means that it is impossible to *exclude* anyone from the use of the concerned good, so that, if it is available for one individual, it is necessarily so for others. Nonrivalry means that individuals are not rivals in the use of the good: the use of this good by an individual does not reduce what is available for others. For instance, if national defence services are produced by a state, one cannot exclude any citizen from the benefit of this protection, and on the other hand, the fact that a citizen is protected does not diminish the protection of others.

It is generally assumed that free competition would not lead to an optimum because nobody would have an interest in producing a good of this type. Since no one can be excluded from the use of the so-called public good, at the moment it is produced, no one is induced to pay for it, because everyone is relying on others to bear the cost of the expenditure in question. Each seeks to behave as a 'stowaway'. But if all citizens behave in this way, the good in question is not produced, or will be produced in insufficient quantities, although it would be in the interest of all that it be produced. In these circumstances, the free entry on the market does not meet the needs of people and does not achieve the best resource allocation. It would be preferable that the state be a monopolist producer of the good in question and that it require citizens to finance it through taxation: this is necessary to prevent them from behaving as 'stowaways'.

This theory seems perfectly coherent and it would therefore be a serious limitation to the general principle of free competition. But it has in fact only the appearance of consistency. It may be noted that there is no reason to prohibit entry into a market for the production of public goods, since it is precisely argued that private producers would not produce this good or would produce it in insufficient quantities. The fact that the state takes a production in charge should therefore not involve prohibiting others to produce it also, that is, to compete.

On another hand, the public goods theory is itself extremely questionable. The justification for a noncompetitive production of a public good consists in preventing certain individuals, located on a national territory, from acting as stowaways. But if they feel that the so-called public good that they are compelled to finance is not good for them, or that it is even an evil, there is no justification for saying that the monopolist and compulsory production of the public good allows *all people* to be in a better situation. Let us take again the example of national defence. An individual who is a conscientious objector will not consider a benefit the fact that he has to give up personal consumption to pay taxes in order to finance public armaments. Those who prefer a conventional defence will be dissatisfied with having to pay for atomic defence, etc. This means that it is probably impossible to find a good that meets perfectly the above definition, according to which everyone would be happier by a compulsory monopolist production rather than by using one's freedom of contract.

The very idea that one can produce resources for which there is no rivalry between users is questionable. These resources would indeed be 'free goods' the availability of which is such that, specifically, the problem of their production does not arise. This is the case with air. Because of its overabundance relative to demand, it is not necessary to produce it – even less by a monopolistic firm. But as soon as resources are scarce, they are necessarily at the origin of rivalries. As we have said, procedures have to be implemented to decide on the use of these resources by some or by others. There are, however, only two procedures: coercion or free exchange. Contrary to its basic assumptions, the public goods theory consists in saying that certain goods for which there are rivalries must be liable to coercive procedures and not to free exchange procedures. But it is wrongly alleged that certain goods, because they have supposedly the characteristics of public goods as defined in an *a priori* theory, cannot be subject to free trade procedures. It would be more correct to say that, in certain circumstances – sometimes numerous – the holders of legal power, producers of public goods under coercion, want to adopt the procedures necessary to prohibit stowaway behaviours. In other words, the existence of public goods can be explained by an analysis of the mechanisms of power and political systems. It does not imply that there could be natural limits to the working of free competition.

Similar remarks can be made about 'externalities', which are often considered a justification for the limitation of competitive procedures. An (positive or negative) externality can be defined as the nondesired and not-requested effect on someone of an human act, made either by another individual or by several individuals linked by contracts. For instance, one may say that the construction of a road can cause negative environmental externalities, or positive externalities if the value of properties located in the vicinity of the road is thus increased. One will then draw the consequence that free entry on the road market would not achieve a social optimum because the economic calculation of the producer, of their suppliers, and of their customers does not take these externalities into account. It should therefore be necessary either that the state takes charge of the construction of a road – which would not be profitable from a narrow accounting perspective, but which could create positive external effects on some people – or that it prevents the free entry of a road producer because of the supposed existence of negative externalities.

In reality, virtually all human actions have consequences for others. If I wear a tie that is disliked by those I meet, I produce a negative externality. If I wear a tie that they like, I create a positive externality. Does this mean that the state must decide the tie I wear or prohibit the free sale and purchase of ties because of the external effects that may occur? It is clear that the generality of externalities is such that it could lead to a ban on any free act because of possible negative externalities. The only real problem is not to look for cases in which one should remove contractual freedom and freedom to act, but to find which are the respective rights of each person and which are the rights that individuals want to define. Thus probably nobody considers it important to decide contractually the wearing of a tie. But if ever the owner of a coffee shop decided to prohibit the entry in his establishment of those who have red ties, because the negative externality that he would suffer would not be compensated by the gain brought by a client, it is his absolute right. It is therefore not justified to deny the existence of externalities – which actually are the simple expression of the fact that the members of a society are necessarily interdependent – but it is justified to deny that they can clarify in any way the debate about competition and that they can help to determine necessary limits to free competition.

This does not mean, on another hand, that all human interactions have to be made through contracts. Often, people find that it is cheaper to use other procedures. This is the explanation provided by Ronald Coase for the existence of firms that may be analyzed as places of social cooperation submitted not to the order of competition but to a kind of internal planning. As he wrote,[2] 'in a competitive system there would be an optimum of planning since a firm, that little planned society, could only continue to exist if it performed its co-ordination function at a lower cost than would be incurred if it were achieved by means of market transactions and also at a lower cost than this same function could be performed by another firm. To have an efficient economic system it is necessary not only to have markets but also areas of planning within organizations of the appropriate size. What this mix should be we find as a result of competition'. We should not forget that even if one thinks, as does Ronald Coase, that there is a planning system within a firm, it is not based on coercion. Moreover, a firm can be defined as a set of contracts and, from this point of view, competition exists for the signatories of contracts.[3] Thus, employees are always potentially subject to competition from those who are likely to replace them, whether they are already in the firm or are outside. Similarly, the entrepreneur is subject to competition from other entrepreneurs who are likely to offer to his or her employees a more attractive contract. Competition can therefore be considered the core of economic life, at least as far as freedom to act does prevail.

A comprehensive approach to competition

So far we have implicitly considered competition only as regards the production of what is called goods and services, although referring to 'public goods' already allowed us to go beyond this framework. But could it not be considered that the notion of competition goes far beyond this, and that it constitutes a general organisation principle of human societies? As is stressed by Viktor Vanberg,[4] competition allows solution of three fundamental problems of any human organization:

- *The problem of incentives*: How can one ensure that individuals act in a way that is beneficial to others? Competition induces people to provide the best products at the lowest price, so as to satisfy consumers. As Adam Smith wrote in a famous phrase: 'It is not from the benevolence of the butcher, the brewer, or the baker that we expect our dinner, but from their regard to their own interest.'
- *The problem of disseminating power*: When competition exists, buyers enjoy a greater freedom of choice and they are more independent from producers.[5]
- *The problem of information*: Competition provides not only a way to best use information which is scattered among the many members of a society, but, in addition, it encourages individuals to seek new information and new ideas, so as to be 'competitive'. As Viktor Vanberg wrote, "market competition is a

knowledge-creation process or a 'process of exploration',[6] it is an open-ended evolutionary process that allows for, and provides incentives for, continuous and countless efforts to come up with better problem-solutions than those that are currently available. It is a process that facilitates adaptation in a world in which our knowledge and the problems we face change in ways that can never be fully anticipated, a process that, for these very reasons, by necessity 'always leads into the unknown'.

Because all problems of social organisation– and not only those that it is customary to call 'economic problems' – involve the creation of knowledge, and because competition is the most effective means for this purpose, it constitutes an essential organizing principle in all human activities.

Let us look, for instance, at the role that competition can play in the functioning of state systems. They are typically constructed from organizational concepts opposed to the principle of competition, although it can be said that rival political parties are competing in elections, that bureaucrats in an administration are competing for promotions, and so on. In other words, a certain degree of *internal* competition (or rivalry) exists necessarily, even though a large number of operating rules limit the working of competition, for example those governing civil servants (automatic rules for promotion, impossibility of firing, etc.). But we will rather consider here the possibility of an *external* competition, that is, competition between public organizations.

Competition is imperfect on the political market because the electoral process consists in determining who will be the beneficiaries of the state monopoly. Certainly, political parties are competing for the sole reason that there is always competition to appropriate scarce resources. But the fact remains that there is no free entry on the public market. Indeed, once the elections have been won by a group of people, citizens are obliged to accept the 'basket' of taxes and public goods offered to them by the winning coalition and they cannot apply to another producer of baskets of taxes and public goods.

Competition in this area would mean that each citizen can freely choose the public producer who would propose to him or her the taxes and the public services which he or she would consider as optimal. We can call this assumption 'functional federalism', since the criterion to delimit governments would not be territorial but functional.

When one talks about competition between states or competition between governments, one refers to a situation in which competition is less perfect than in the above hypothesis. Each state enjoys a legal, regulatory, and taxing monopoly on a given territory, but citizens can freely move – or, at least, move part of their activities – and therefore they may choose the state under which they prefer to live.

Competition between states may therefore take various forms that are more or less close to what constitutes competition in other markets, those of which it is generally said that they are 'competitive'. Moreover, it may concern more or less important parts of the activities carried out by states: One can introduce competition between tax systems, between laws and regulations, between public services. Let us take for example the case of the production of law.

It has two aspects. There is first the production of rules *within a given legal system*. Thus, there are two major systems of law production: The legal system and the judicial system, that is, approximately, the continental or French system and the Anglo-Saxon system (common law). In the legal system, law is produced by a public monopoly, the Parliament, and law is defined pragmatically not by its role in social adjustment processes, but simply as the rule produced by the Parliament (or the leader in an autocratic system). A Parliament is supposed to know and to implement the 'best' rules of law, that is, those that best meet the needs of the members of a society, more specifically the country in which Parliament has this monopoly. Saying that there is a monopoly is saying that there is no freedom of entry into the market. It is the case in modern legal systems, since nobody can come and compete with the Parliament by claiming to produce better laws and no one can choose the rules under which he or she lives in relation with others.

In a judicial system, on the contrary, the law is not made, it is *discovered*. On the occasion of concrete cases, the judicial system *expresses law*, inspired by the general principles of law and jurisprudence. There is, from this point of view, a certain degree of competition in the law market since a judge may produce a rule of law by modifying a jurisprudence or by creating a new jurisprudence for a new case that appears.

That is why an author such as Bruno Leoni[7] was able to compare the judicial system to the market process. Similarly to the working of a market in which competition *allows one to discover* the needs of everyone, a jurisprudential system gradually allows participants to discover the rules of law that are efficient in human interrelationships. Similar to a monopolist who does not perfectly meet the needs of the demanders of a good, the monopolist producer of rights has no means – or possibly no desire – to know if the rules imposed on citizens fit their needs in the best way. As we know, competition is a process of discovery. In a world where information is necessarily imperfect, the absence of competition makes the development of human activities more difficult, regardless of the precise nature of these activities. The problem is the same whether one produce tomatoes, books, or law rules.

One could obviously push the competition assumption to the extreme by assuming that anyone would have the right to become a judge, the more or less good quality of the judgments leading through a *competitive process* to select the best judges or those who would be affiliated with a judicial system, a network of judges, considered as making probably more efficient and fairer judgments. This assumption is not absurd because this is actually the way by which arbitration is working and its growing success is an indication of the usefulness of competition in such a field.

It would be possible to use again, as regards law, arguments that we have already seen. In fact, the argument usually advanced in favour of the existence of a monopoly for the production of law is based on the idea that it is in the interest of 'all people' – which, in reality, means those who are located in a territory arbitrarily determined and called a nation – to have a single law. It is clear that a very great multiplicity of law systems would be inefficient, as would be a too great multiplicity of currencies or of telecommunication systems. But what is the optimal number of law systems? We do not know, and only competition would enable us to know. It is obvious that, if there was complete freedom of entry into the market for law, some law systems – maybe even one at the limit – would be selected by use as being the most efficient and the best adapted to the concrete circumstances of time and place. From this point of view we can say again that competition is a process of discovery. Instead of determining *a priori* the desirable number of law systems, as is currently the case – with the consequence that some, strangely enough, are used for a very large population and others for very small populations – or instead of determining *a priori* the number of firms that must produce computers, TV broadcasting, or atomic power plants, it is obviously preferable to *find* the optimal number of producers in each field and its likely evolution thanks to a competitive process: free entry. If one can really gain, at a given time, by reducing the number of producers of a particular good or service, people are able to notice it and to implement the necessary procedures to achieve this optimal number.

The other aspect of law competition is competition *between law systems*. This problem does not really arise if there are real jurisprudential systems, in particular, of course, if there is freedom of entry into a judicial system. In this case, in fact, there is freedom of choice, both as regards the users of law who can choose their judicial system (their court or their arbitrator), and the producers of law who compete one with the other to produce the best rules of law and the most efficient and least expensive judgment procedures.

But let us assume that there is – as it is generally the case in the modern world – a situation in which law is produced by national monopolies, each law being compulsory and being used only in the territory reserved to a given parliamentary monopoly. Cannot some limited competition be introduced? As an answer to this question, let us take the example of the European area.

A certain degree of law competition already exists as far as individuals are free to move or to move resources from one country to another, that is, from a legal space to another. They can then decide the location of their activities on the basis of the advantages – from their own viewpoint – of each of the existing law systems. But, of course, as law systems have a territorial base and as they are not the only elements taken into account in a decision of location, law competition remains, from this point of view, limited.

Competition is strengthened if a rule can have some applicability beyond its original national space. This is why one can consider, as a reinforcement of law competition, the famous decision of 1979 called Cassis de Dijon, by which the Court of Justice of the European Communities has admitted that, for a good produced in a country of the European Economic Community in accordance with the standards of this country, the import of this good in another country could not be forbidden under the pretext that it was not complying with the standards of this second country. In other words, the standards laid down in France for the Cassis de Dijon are applicable in the territory of other European countries for the same product. The principle of mutual recognition of standards has been acknowledged for the time being in the European Union and it is an important example of law competition. But this competition is still limited compared to a more extreme case, which one could imagine.

There would be, in fact, a true law competition if one could freely use in a country rules and laws adopted in another country. Thus, to take again the case of standards, competition would be even greater if, for instance, any German or English producer could freely choose to use standards which are legal in France or Greece and, *a fortiori*, if the standards were of private origin.

From a more general point of view one can therefore say that there are two concepts diametrically opposed of European integration. One is to improve the working of markets – all markets – by increasing competition, that is, by removing all barriers to the freedom of choice. The other consists, on the contrary, in creating public European monopolies. The first one corresponds to the generalization of what had been called the Common Market: freedom of trade and production for goods, standards and rules, currencies, factors of production, etc. The second corresponds to the multiplication of so-called harmonization decisions – for instance as regards taxes or regulations – the adoption of common policies, the centralization of decisions. This distinction is therefore the one that exists between the spontaneous differentiation of activities and their forced homogenization. As we saw previously, the great merit of competition is precisely that it incites to diversification. Therefore, if one wishes that European integration can better meet the needs of Europeans, should not the first approach be adopted – increasing competition in Europe in all areas?

This does not mean that one must develop 'competition policies', at least if it means the control of monopolies, cartels, and dominant positions. As at the national level, a paradox arises from the fact that one aims at fighting against false monopolies and that, at the same time, one creates true monopolies. Moreover, it is wrong to believe that the 'harmonization of the conditions of competition', so often claimed, is necessary for competition to prevail. As seen previously, competition has precisely the merit that it induces producers to diversify their conditions of production and to remain 'competitive' despite the existing differences in their environments.

Extending competition to the field of public activities would bring, inter alia, two benefits, consistent with what could be expected in general from competition:

- It gives to individuals more freedom of choice and it reduces their subordination to state power. Indeed, as a contrast, let us imagine a world where all laws, all taxes would be the same over the entire surface of the globe. If an individual believed that he is despoiled by this system, he could not choose another one. Certainly, one may say, he still has the right to vote, if the global monopolistic state is democratic. He would thus have the hope of changing, thanks to his strength of conviction and his vote, the decisions taken by the World Government. But this hope is quite weak, one might easily agree, since the democratic rule implies only that the rights of the majority are recognised.
- Second, intergovernmental competition can encourage public authorities to adjust their decisions so as to better serve citizens; otherwise they might see a brain drain, or, at least, the flight of certain resources. Moreover, the

multiplicity of experiences can improve the quality of decisions, at least if one assumes that governments are inclined to effectively pursue such an aim.

Intergovernmental competition is therefore more efficient as states are smaller, and this is why one should even be in favour of competition between city councils. In fact, competition between governments is very different from competition between entrepreneurs, because of its territorial characteristic: even if there is competition between the authorities of different territories, each authority has a monopoly on its territory. The cost to be borne by people to migrate from one territory to another is higher than the cost incurred when shifting from one producer to another on a market, and this cost is obviously the larger the wider is the area on which there is a territorial public monopoly. However, it can be hoped, for instance, that the moving of marginal taxpayers can exert a pressure on governments.

Of course, we meet, concerning the idea of intergovernmental competition, the objection already encountered about public goods. If there is a strong intergovernmental competition, it is frequently said, an individual can escape his 'civic duty' by fleeing to another jurisdiction. It is also stressed that there is the risk that some people will become stowaways, benefiting from public services on a territory and paying their taxes on another. However, we know that the argument concerning a behaviour of stowaway is debatable and, moreover, a problem of this kind can always be solved by a better definition of the tax base and/or a better definition of the goods produced by public authorities.

One should not expect, however, from competition between public authorities results identical to those that can be expected from competition among private organizations. In fact, one of the key roles of competition is to establish a 'discovery process'. Competition makes it possible to provide relevant information to responsible producers who are therefore encouraged to make the best use of this information. What happens with public organisations?

Let us suppose that the States and other public authorities are benevolent, that they are eager to improve the lives of citizens. The fact remains, however, that there is a problem with the complexity of information. Thus, it is difficult to understand the link between a tax system and economic activity. When the causal relationships are complex, an intellectual effort to understand the working of a system is certainly more important than experience. If, for example, the citizens of two neighbouring states enjoy a different degree of prosperity, experience alone is not enough to assign these differences to tax systems, regulations, climatic differences, or natural resources. The information content of competition is therefore probably much smaller than in the case of competition between goods and specific services.

If one believes, on the contrary, that those who are in charge of state activities are not benevolent, but that they pursue their own goals at the expense of citizens, they will precisely seek to protect themselves from a possible competition from other states, for example by limiting migrations or expanding their territory by conquest or political unification. There is in fact in this case a contradiction, insofar as interstate competition means somehow the freedom to enter into the 'coercion market.'

Notes

1 Smith (1776), quoted by Viktor Vanberg (1993), IV: l, pp. 3–28. We owe much to this article for some parts of the present chapter.
2 Coase (1991).
3 One may refer to our text "Firm or market: Where are the limits?", Chapter 2 of our book, Salin (2015).
4 Viktor Vanberg, (1993).
5 Even if, at some point of time, there is only one producer of a good – for instance, for a new product – fearing the arrival of a competitor induces a producer to satisfy his customers.
6 Hayek (1978).
7 Leoni (1961).

Part II
Free trade

Introduction

The liberalization of trade is a major fact of the evolution of the world in recent decades. It arose, on the one hand, as the creation of regional organizations – of which the European Union is obviously one of the best-known examples – and on the other hand, as efforts to alleviate or eliminate barriers to trade at the global level. But this evolution is accompanied in some countries by a growing questioning of what is commonly called globalization. It is therefore particularly important in our time to understand the consequences of free trade and the reasons why it is desirable. But studying free trade also implies necessarily a detailed and precise examination of the arguments of those who fear global liberalization. This is one of the aims pursued in the second part of the present book.

Free trade can be defined in a negative way as a situation in which obstacles of institutional nature to trade do not exist. It does not, of course, involve the removal of geographical, physical, or linguistic barriers. Symmetrically, protectionism is the set of measures of State origin that limit, prohibit, control, or influence international trade. Protectionism is thus the result of a public power of coercion that interferes with exchange processes based on the free will of those who are directly concerned by these exchanges.

Protectionism therefore introduces discriminations in trade according to the fact that it takes place between residents of the same country or between residents of a country and residents of foreign countries. In this sense, protectionism is a regulatory nationalism.

It is customary to consider protectionism mainly as a policy concerning trade in commodities. In reality, as we will see, one can give a more extensive interpretation of protectionism, including, for instance, the flows of factors of production.

Protectionist practices are old. They are also used throughout the world. Does it mean that protectionism is justified? Only a rigorous analysis makes it possible to answer this question. We give the main lines of this analysis in the present book: Chapters 7 to 9 will first analyze freedom of trade, attempting to understand the implications and modalities of protectionism, and comparing protectionist situations with free trade situations.

We will then arrive at a paradox: protectionism seems harmful and yet it is generalised. Should we therefore admit that, despite the general statements that are opposed to protectionism, certain specific situations may justify it? There are actually a whole series of arguments in favour of protectionism. We will look at them in Chapter 10. But in reality, protectionism is essentially an institutional and social phenomenon resulting from the game of political forces (Chapter 11).

Despite these forces opposed to free trade, it is possible to make progress in the direction of liberalization. We will study the processes in Chapter 12 before giving some historical examples in Chapter 13.

7 Justifications for free trade

Human beings differ one from the other, both as regards their productive capacities and their specific needs. This simple statement explains why trade does exist and allows understanding of why it is beneficial. We will first study trade between individuals. The general principles we will draw from this study will allow us, by a simple extension, to understand trade between different sets of individuals, for instance those who constitute a nation and who are, therefore, doing what is called *international* trade.

Trade between individuals

To understand the phenomenon of trade, let us first imagine a very simplified world where there are only two individuals, Peter and Paul, and two goods, wine and wheat. If trade is not possible between these two individuals, for one reason or another, each will have to meet his own needs thanks to corresponding productions. Let us suppose that Peter is more skillful than Paul for both productions. Thus, in a day's work, he is able to produce 4 pounds of wheat or 2 pints of wine, whereas Paul can produce only 1 pound of wheat or 1 pint of wine.

Each of them chooses to distribute time between the two activities according to their preferences. For instance, let us suppose that Peter has decided to use his time such that, on average, he produces every day 2 pounds of wheat and 1 pint of wine (which means that he devotes the same period of time to each of these activities). If he wants to change the structure of his production, for instance to consume more wine, he must abandon the production of 2 pounds of wheat to obtain one additional pint of wine. One may call the ratio between the quantities produced of each item per unit of time the 'individual transformation rate'. For Peter, this rate is equal to 1/2, meaning that he can substitute the production of 1 pint of wine for the production of 2 pounds of wheat or vice versa. For Paul, the individual transformation rate equals 1/1: To produce one additional pound of wheat he must give up one pint of wine, to produce one additional pint of wine he must give up one pound of wheat.

However, let us suppose now that trade becomes suddenly possible between these two individuals. A superficial view of the situation could lead one to think that Peter will replace Paul in the two activities, as he is more productive in these two areas.[1] However, what will explain the exchange and productive activities of each individual is not the fact that their productivity – their production per unit time – is different in absolute terms (Peter being more productive than Paul for all productions). It is the fact that there are *relative* differences in productivity. Although Peter is more productive than Paul for the production of wine, he is still *relatively* more productive for the production of wheat.

Given that Peter does not have unlimited time resources, he would waste his time if he wanted to produce everything he needs himself, while he can have recourse to exchange. To produce one additional pint of wine Peter must sacrifice 2 pounds of wheat, whereas Paul must sacrifice only one pound of wheat. It is this difference that explains the interest in exchange, and which allows us to understand why exchange will take place. It is in the interest of both individuals to specialise in the production of one of the two goods, to sell a part of his production and thus to obtain the other good. In our example, Peter will have an interest in specializing in the production of wheat – for which he is relatively more productive – and in buying wine against wheat, if he can get more than one pint of wine for 2 pounds of wheat. Similarly, Paul has an interest in specializing in the production of wine if he can get more than 1 pound of wheat against 1 pint of wine. It is clear that these wants are reconcilable.

Let us call a market price the quantity of a good that is obtained against another in an exchange. If, for example, two potential partners reach an agreement for a market price of 1/1.5 – they exchange 1 pint of wine against 1.5 pounds of wheat – this exchange is beneficial for both partners. To obtain 1 pint of wine, Peter must give up 1.5 pounds of wheat, while he ought to give up 2 pounds of wheat if he had wanted to produce his wine himself. Paul gets 1.5 pounds of wheat by sacrificing 1 pint of wine, while he would have obtained only 1 pound of wheat if he had wanted to produce his wheat himself.

Each of the two traders agrees to this exchange, although they would be free not to do so. It is the proof that the exchange brings to each of them a gain we cannot measure, but the existence of which is certain. We cannot measure such a gain because it is subjective. If Peter agrees to sell 1.5 pounds of wheat to get one pint of wine, it is because the usefulness *for him* of one pint of wine is greater than the usefulness of 1.5 pounds of wheat; if not he would not have done this exchange. For Paul, exactly the opposite is happening: the usefulness *for him* of one pint of wine is less than the usefulness of 1.5 pounds of wheat. The exchange was born from these differences in the assessment of the subjective and relative usefulness of goods. Which are the reasons for these differences? They can come from differences on the side of production, for instance from the fact that two individuals have different *relative* productive capacities (Peter being relatively more productive in the production of wheat than in the production of wine). But they can also come from differences in *relative* preferences and needs (Peter being relatively more willing to consume wine).

The precise reasons for this exchange do not matter much. We know in an irrefutable way that, as far as differences between individuals exist – either from the point of view of their productive capacities, or from the point of view of their preferences – there are trade opportunities and there is a gain due to trade. This gain is subjective and thus not measurable, but it is nonetheless very concrete. But on the other hand, the values exchanged during a transaction – the values expressed in terms of market prices of what is purchased and what is simultaneously sold – are strictly equivalent. Suppose we choose to express the price of the two goods in terms of wheat – that is, wheat serves as a standard unit of measure – and that 1 pint of wine is worth 1.5 pounds of wheat. If, for instance, Peter sells 15 pounds of wheat and buys 10 pints of wine, the 'value' – expressed in terms of pounds of wheat – of what he sells is 15 and the 'value' of what he buys is also equal to 15 (since 1 pint of wine 'is worth' 1.5 pounds of wheat on the market, i.e. in the exchange). Thus there is an equality between the exchanged values, expressed in terms of a same standard of value (wheat in our example). But these exchanged values – which are indeed measurable – should not be confused with subjective values, corresponding to the assessment of the usefulness of the different goods by an individual. Although the measured value (or worth) of what is purchased by Peter is equal to the measured value of what he sells, he makes a gain, since the subjective value (for him and him only) of what he buys is greater than the subjective value of what he sells, otherwise he would have not completed the transaction in question. The situation is symmetric for Paul (equality of market values, but inequality of subjective values).

Thus, the accounting equivalence of the exchanged values should not hide this fundamental phenomenon that an exchange is *productive*, in the sense that it is creating (subjective) value, meaning that it allows the two partners in the exchange to reach situations they prefer. To paraphrase: when an exchange is possible and permitted, an individual could decide not to exchange actually. If he freely decides to do an exchange, it is necessarily because it is beneficial for him. This is a logical consequence of the fact that individuals are rational, meaning that they are able to determine their own aims and able to choose the best means to reach them.

International trade

The above statements about the creation of value through exchange provides the fundamental justification for free trade: If an exchange takes place freely, we must be convinced, without even having to ask them, that it is good for all the partners in the exchange. This is true when considering the exchange between two individuals as in the example above, but also when considering the exchanges between individuals who belong to different sets of individuals, for instance those that constitute countries. A country can be defined as a set of individuals located on a given territory and subject to a system of power. If the power in question does not prevent free exchanges between the set of individuals who constitute its country and the other sets of individuals (or the other countries), one says that free trade prevails, this term being generally used to characterise trade between residents of different countries – the so-called international trade – and not trade between individuals of the same country. The opposite situation – the one in which specific constraints are imposed on international exchanges – corresponds to protectionism.

Let us suppose for the sake of simplicity that there are two countries in the world, A and B, and two products, wheat and wine. If, on average, the inhabitants of country A buy wine and sell wheat, it is because:

- They are *relatively* more efficient as a whole[2] to produce wheat rather than wine compared to the inhabitants of country B;
- and/or they prefer relatively wine to wheat in comparison with the inhabitants of country B.

The nature of the problem is obviously not changed if we introduce a currency in the reasoning. It serves both as an intermediary in exchange and a store of value, but we are concerned only with the first of these roles here.[3] Thus, the previous transaction consisting of trading wheat against wine will be separated into two transactions, one to exchange wheat for money and the other consisting of trading wine against money. Peter, for instance, will sell 15 pounds of wheat (to Paul or to another person) against a quantity of money worth – in terms of market prices – 15 pounds of wheat. And he will use this money to buy (from Paul or someone else) 10 pints of wine which are worth 15 pounds of wheat in terms of market prices.

One can also imagine – as is happening nowadays – that, instead of defining a currency in terms of a certain quantity of commodities,[4] one has given an arbitrary name to a currency, for example the euro (€). If one uses the currency as the numeraire (standard of value) – and not only as an intermediary in exchange and a store of value – and if, at a given moment of time, 1 pint of wine = €1, it will result that 1.5 pounds of wheat = €1. The transaction which had been imagined above will then be done as follows: Peter sells 15 pounds of wheat, with a monetary value of €10 (in terms of market prices expressed in currency euro), against a sum of money equal to €10 (that is, there is equivalence in the exchange between market values, expressed in monetary terms). Then he will resell these €10 against 10 pints of wine, the monetary value of which is €10 (in terms of market prices expressed in currency euro). He will have finally traded, as above in a barter economy, 15 pounds of wheat against 10 pints of wine.

One can record these operations by using accounting entries in the transaction account below:

Transaction account of Peter			
Purchases (–)		*Sales (+)*	
Money	€10	Wheat	€10
Wine	€10	Money	€10

It may be recalled that it is usual to write a minus sign for the purchase part of a transaction and a plus sign for the sale part. It must be clear that it is a simple writing convention and that the contrary convention could just as well be decided. A drawback of this convention is that it induces the misconception that purchases represent something 'negative'. When one calls the purchases 'imports', because the supplier is a foreign resident, it may be wrongly inferred – because of the use of the minus sign – that it is 'bad' to import. Yet we have seen that purchases are inseparable from sales and that an individual purchases to get an extra satisfaction. In this sense, what brings satisfaction, what is desired, is the 'purchase' part (the import) of his transaction; and what represents a sacrifice for him is the 'sale' (export) part, since he must renounce using himself what he sells to others.

If we write the balance for each item (transactions on wheat, wine, and money), we get the following account:

Transaction account of Peter			
Purchases (–)		Sales (+)	
Wine	€10	Wheat	€10

This account reflects the fact that ultimately Peter traded €10 of wine against €10 of wheat. If one shifts back from a monetary standard of value to a wheat standard, and since €1 = 1.5 pounds of wheat and 1 pint of wine = €1, one has exchanged 10 pints of wine (worth 15 pounds of wheat) against 15 pounds of wheat. Even if provisionally Peter has traded wheat for money, what he wished to do ultimately was to exchange wheat against wine.

The nature of the problem does not change if one considers a larger number of goods. It does not change either if one considers a greater number of people. For example, we can imagine that the individuals Peter, James, and John constitute what is called a 'country', because they are on the same territory, defined more or less arbitrarily. They exchange among themselves and they exchange with 'foreigners'. If one establishes the transaction account of the set of people that they constitute, that is, the account of the transactions they carry out with foreigners, one will obviously find back the feature that we met above, namely the fact that the purchases are equal to the sales (both being expressed in terms of the same monetary or nonmonetary standard of value). This consolidated transaction account is written, for example, as follows:

Consolidated transaction account of Peter, James, and John (country A)			
Purchases		Sales	
Money	€10	Wheat	€10
Wheat	€5	Money	€5
Wine	€10	Money	€10
Money	€5	Wine	€5

This example implies that all the individuals in country A are not specialised in the production of wheat, since there are also sales of wine abroad. But on the average there is a specialization of country A – of its inhabitants – in wheat production. If one writes only the balance for each item, one obtains the following account:

Consolidated transaction account of Peter, James, and John (country A)

Purchases		Sales	
Wine	€5	Wheat	€5

Oddly enough, one gives a specific name to this account when it concerns transactions between a group of individuals within the territory of a country and individuals in the rest of the world: one calls this account a *balance of payments*. Of course, the balance of payments we consider here is very simplified. In particular, we have not introduced the exchange of securities and various financial claims. Moreover, we have assumed that traders considered money only as an intermediary in trade, which means that they quickly get rid of the currency that they get thanks to their sales so as to purchase other commodities. However, one may wish to accumulate money cash-balances. For the time being, however, we will remain within the framework of our simplified assumptions (absence of transactions on securities and financial claims, money playing only the role of an intermediary in trade), so as to focus on the analysis of protectionism – what we will do in the following chapter – since protectionism is mainly related to transactions in commodities. But if one removes these simplifying assumptions – which we will do in Chapter 10 – the analysis of protectionism is not modified.

Notes

1 One is doing a similar reasoning when claiming, for instance, that a 'disadvantaged' country has nothing to exchange. We will see that this idea is erroneous.
2 Of course, it may occur that some inhabitants of country A are relatively more able to produce wine than wheat and are thus specialised in this production. But the assumption above is only to assume that *overall* the inhabitants of A are relatively more able to produce wheat.
3 As regards the roles of a currency one may refer to our book, Salin (2016).
4 It should be noted that money has originally taken the form of certain amounts of commodities, for instance copper, gold, salt, etc.

8   The effects of protectionism

As we have already said, protectionism is the set of public means of coercion to prohibit or to limit the purchase of goods abroad by the residents of a country or to increase their price. Producers in the concerned country are thus protected against competition from foreign producers.

The main protectionist measures include:

- Customs duties or tariffs: A customs duty is a specific tax on imported goods or some of them. The duty, calculated as a percentage of the value of the concerned good, is called an *ad valorem* duty. If it is a fixed rate per unit of a commodity or per amount (for instance per pound or inch), it is called a specific duty.
- Quotas: A quota is a quantitative measure that consists in limiting the amount of goods the import of which is authorised during a specified period. Any import beyond a quota is prohibited.
- Administrative measures according to which imports are subject to prior authorizations (licensing of imports), or certain imports are prohibited (e.g., products considered as dangerous) or certain standards have to be respected (e.g., for technical reasons, security, health, etc.). The protectionist intent – the desire to protect domestic producers against foreign producers – does not necessarily exist when measures of this kind are decided, but their protectionist nature is not less real.
- Other measures may have a protectionist effect. We examine them in detail in Chapter 9.

The analysis of customs duties

Let us first assume that a country, for example called Brit, is in a barter economy and that there are only two traded goods, wine and wheat. In a situation of free trade, this country – its inhabitants (Brits) – buys in each period 10 pints of wine and sells 15 pounds of wheat (as in the example given in Chapter 7), which means that the Brits are specialised in the production of wheat and the rest of the world in the production of wine. This specialisation of productive activities allows the inhabitants of each country to benefit from a higher standard of living, as we have seen previously. On the other hand, it can reasonably be assumed that Brit is small compared with the rest of the world, which implies that relative prices between goods are mainly determined by the supplies and demands of the inhabitants in the rest of the world. One trades, for example, 1 pint of wine against 1.5 pound of wheat. Taking into account this given world relative price, the Brits wish to sell each day 15 pounds of wheat and to buy 10 pints of wine, what they do actually, to the greatest satisfaction of all.

But all of a sudden let us imagine that the leader of Brits, Interventionnix, using his monopolist powers of coercion, imposes a customs duty on imports – on purchases made abroad – at a rate of 25%. We do not care about his purposes for the time being, but we will have the opportunity to discuss them later.

What will happen? Outside, when providing one pint of wine, a seller will wish to get 1.5 pounds of wheat, since that is the price of wine in terms of wheat. If the Brits import (buy) 10 pints of wine, they must provide 15 pounds of wheat. But Interventionnix will charge 25% on purchases at the crossing of the border, that is, 2.5 pints of wine. Against 15 pounds of wheat that they deliver, Brit importers will therefore obtain 7.5 pints of wine and no longer 10. In Brit, the relative price between wine and wheat resulting from international trade (after payment of taxes) is now 1/2 instead of 1/1.5: one exchanges 1 pint of wine against 2 pounds of wheat.

It is obviously inconceivable that there be different relative prices inside Brit depending on whether one has recourse to domestic or international exchange. The new relative price (1/2) therefore prevails inside. We can then determine the various implications of this specific tax levied on imports, called a customs duty:

The first consequence is an indisputable overall consequence: there is a loss of well-being for the people of Brit, as far as the benefits of free trade and interindividual specialization are now limited or even deleted. Thus, let us imagine that the conditions of production in Brit are such that the 'relative price in isolation' between wine and wheat is equal to 1/2 (1 pint of wine against 2 pounds of wheat) in the absence of international trade (situation of autarchy). In the example that we took, it is no more profitable to exchange with foreign producers: by doing an international exchange and by paying the duty rate of 25%, a seller of wheat gets no more wine than if he got wine from a national producer. With a lower customs duty, exchanges would remain profitable, but the gain due to exchange would, however, be lower than in the case of free trade. Protectionism necessarily implies a less good use of productive resources. This is an obvious fact: one wins when moving from autarchy to free trade, and one necessarily loses when taking back the direction of autarchy.

The overall loss is unevenly distributed and some inhabitants of the protectionist country derive even a gain from protection. When we had analyzed the benefits of free trade, we had assumed for simplicity that Peter was able to produce, with the same factors of production, 1 pint of wine or 2 pounds of wheat. We had concluded that he had an interest in abandoning the production of wine if he could exchange 1 pint of wine against 1.5 pounds of wheat. But the real situations are more complex. First, one can imagine that there are in the country various producers, more or less able to produce wheat (those whose transformation rates between wheat and wine are higher or lower than Peter's rate), and we can even assume that Peter is able to use a lower quality land to produce more wheat if its price (in terms of wine) is higher. Thus, when shifting from a situation of autarchy to a situation of free trade – which allows one to obtain wine at lower prices – the less efficient wine producers will progressively abandon wine production to concentrate on the production of wheat, and only efficient wine producers will continue to produce in the country. Conversely, when shifting from a situation of free trade to a situation of protection, the less efficient producers are again able to produce wine. As regards the efficient producers of wine, they have an additional gain, since they can now sell their wine at a higher price (in terms of wheat).

Protection implies a global waste of resources, since they are not used in the most efficient way, but some producers – the producers of wine in our example – benefit from it. But wheat producers are obviously losers in this regime compared to the situation of free trade, since they receive less wine against their wheat. It is therefore important to understand that protection, even if it benefits some people – the producers of protected goods – is harmful for all others. The losses of some people are necessarily greater, in absolute value, than the gains of others, since there is an overall loss, corresponding to the disappearance of the exchange gain: Wine producers cannot obtain a gain without imposing a loss – greater than their gain – on the inhabitants of the country.

It is therefore clear that the advantage granted in one country to a category of producers – those who produce the products protected from outside competition – is obtained at the expense of other producers and of consumers. The reason is that protection implies naturally – and could even be thus defined – a modification of the domestic relative prices, resulting from a state intervention (in the case we are studying, this intervention is a tax called a customs duty or tariff): The introduction of a tariff on imports of wine brings a protection – a privilege – to the domestic producers of wine to the extent that it imposes an additional burden to wheat producers (who may also be consumers of wine). In other words, the positive protection enjoyed by wine producers is inseparable from the negative protection that weighs on wheat producers. Giving a privilege to the first ones is imposing a disadvantage to the latter ones (and imposing a smaller efficiency of production to all the inhabitants of the nation). In the case we consider – where there are only two goods – this conclusion is immediate. And we can also imagine that wheat producers will try vigorously to prevent wine producers from obtaining the privilege in question, because they realise immediately that it is paid by them.

These compulsory transfers of resources are less visible if there are very large numbers of goods. Let us suppose that it is the case and that we are initially in a situation of free trade. Now, at some point, public authorities decide to give a specific benefit to wine producers thanks to a protection in the form of a customs duty. The gain of these producers is necessarily obtained at the expense of all other producers: the price of wine increases in terms of each of the other goods, meaning that one gets less wine in exchange for one unit of each of these other goods. But it is obvious that this effect is more diffuse, more difficult to perceive when there are greater numbers of goods. We will later see that the very existence of protectionism is related to this feature (Chapter 11).

One can interpret the remarks above as a simple application of the traditional theory of monopoly. Indeed, it explains that a monopolist – a producer who is the only producer of a given good on a market – can impose a price higher than would be the case in a situation of competition, so that the loss of consumers is greater, in absolute value, than the gain of the monopolist. In the context of this traditional theory, competition is defined in particular by the fact that there are large numbers of producers in a given market. Now, as we saw in the first part of this book, this definition is questionable because in reality, when competition exists, each producer tries to differentiate from others in producing better and cheaper goods: by getting, thanks to his or her own productive efforts, a (momentary) position of 'monopoly', which in fact is always threatened because it is not protected by coercion.[1] This is why competition must rather be defined as the situation where any producer is free to enter a market. On the other hand, the state has the monopoly of legal coercion and it can thus restrict access to a market. This is what it does when it imposes duties on the import of a product: There is then creation of a monopoly situation – a protection from foreign competition – for the benefit of domestic producers. One may thus find the result of the traditional theory: the gain of the monopolist is at the expense of consumers and the value of this gain is lower, in absolute terms, than the value of their loss. The forced transfer from consumers to producers that is implied by protection is therefore particularly inefficient since it results in a destruction of value.

There is another beneficiary of the protection, the state. This is obvious, since a customs duty is a tax. In the example above, for each imported unit of wine the state levies a tax equal to 25% of the imported value. Of course, the value of the tax can be expressed by using wine or wheat as a standard of value. Furthermore, the tax may be paid in wine or wheat: If the inhabitants of Brit buy 10 pints of wine against 15 pounds of wheat, it is the same for them to give back to the state 2.5 pints of wine or 5 pounds of wheat. If they are paying 2.5 pints of wine, this means that they get 7.5 pints of wine against 15 pounds of wheat (so that the domestic relative price between wine and wheat is equal to 1/2). If they hand over 5 pounds of wheat to the State, this means that, against 10 pints of wine, they must give up 20 pounds of wheat (15 pounds to their foreign partners and 5 pounds to the state): The domestic relative price is thus also equal to 1/2 in this case.

In other words, a customs duty on imports at a rate of 25% can be interpreted in two ways which are perfectly equivalent: one can say that national traders must pay to the state 25% of what they receive from their foreign partners in return for what they sell to them (they sell 15 pounds of wheat, get 10 pints of wine on which they pay 2.5 pints to the state); or it can be said that, to get 10 pints of wine, one must deliver 20 pounds of wheat, of which 25% are given to the state. The internal price being equal to 1/2, the state can still transform into wheat, at this price, the wine it receives as a payment of the tax, or, conversely, exchange wheat against wine. The result is the same for the traders. If they have paid the customs duty in wine, they perhaps got this wine by selling wheat (the domestic price being 1/2, they had to give up 5 pounds of wheat to pay a tax amounting to 2.5 pints of wine).

We thus come to an important conclusion: it is equivalent to levy customs duties on imports or exports. The reason is simple: One cannot separate in a transaction the purchase part and the sale part, so that, in reality, when the state taxes a purchase, it taxes the entire transaction and, therefore, the sale corresponding to this purchase. Thus, when believing that one is taxing imports, one also taxes exports; when believing that one is discouraging imports, one also discourages exports. Unlike what people think in general, protection – under the form, for instance, of a customs duty – does not favor exports over imports, it promotes domestic activities compared to international exchange activities, whether these international activities are imports or exports. This will be a reason for us to explain later (Chapter 10) that it is absurd to impose a protectionist policy on alleged grounds of balance of payments problems.

As protectionism aims at bringing relative prices in international exchange closer to domestic relative prices in isolation, it makes international exchange less desirable. There is a decrease in specialization and in trade. Protectionism does not reduce only imports; it simultaneously reduces exports. At the limit, one goes back to a situation of autarchy (lack of international trade). It may be noted in passing that protectionism becomes even more harmful the lower the economic dimension of a country is. Indeed, the bigger the country the more its relative prices affect international prices. Therefore opening trade changes its relative prices less than in the case of a small country. On the other hand, if a small country had to meet by itself all the needs of its inhabitants, it would necessarily do it in a very inefficient way. This is why the protectionist policies adopted by most of the less developed countries – which are small countries from an economic point of view – are particularly harmful. In contrast, in small countries such as the 'four tigers' of Southeast Asia (Taiwan, South Korea, Singapore, and Hong Kong), one can see the benefits that can be obtained from an opening on foreign countries.[2]

We recalled above that a customs duty is a tax. We can add now that it is a costly way to impose a tax. Of course, there is an administrative cost corresponding not only to the cost of customs services for the public budget but also by the obligations – the cost of which is not recorded statistically – borne by importers (declarations, procedures, controls, delays in delivery, etc.). But beyond this cost – which exists in various degrees for the levying of any tax – there is a specific cost, difficult to measure, that corresponds to the loss of consumer welfare due to the distortions in prices imposed by a protectionist policy.

We assumed implicitly above that the losses due to this tax were fully borne by the nationals of the protectionist country. But it may happen, in fact, that the burden be shared between nationals and foreigners. This is simply the consequence of the fact that protectionism in a country causes a reduction of international trade and, therefore, a reduction of the gain obtained from international exchange by all traders. It brings all countries closer to a situation of autarchy. The inhabitants of a country must bear the effects of protectionism from another country all the more that this latter country is larger and therefore more able to change international relative prices. We will later see a particular application of this idea, known as 'optimum tariff' (Chapter 10).

So far, we have measured relative prices in terms of a real standard of value, that is, for instance, in terms of pounds of wheat. But if a currency exists, it can be used as a standard of value; one can measure the prices of goods in terms of monetary units. Let us suppose that there is a currency called the euro (€) and let us assume that at some given time there is the following monetary price: 1.5 pound of wheat = €1. Knowing the relative price between wheat and euro, one can switch from one standard of value to another: For instance one may shift from a real price of wine in terms of pounds of wheat (for example, 1 pint of wine = 1.5 pound of wheat) to a monetary price in euros (1 pint of wine = €1), or vice versa. Relative prices between wheat and wine are obviously not changed by this change of standard of value. In other words, the introduction of a monetary standard does not alter the reasoning developed above. If it is assumed that there is a single currency in the world, for example the euro, a country imports the goods the prices of which in isolation, expressed in euros, are higher than the foreign prices, and it exports the goods the prices of which in isolation, expressed in euros, are lower than the foreign prices.

We will see later (Chapter 10) what can be said when considering a currency not only as a potential standard of value, but primarily as a specific good providing specific services. The theory of protection we have just presented will be unaffected so far.

The analysis of import quotas

Let us recall what a customs duty is: it consists in modifying the prices of traded goods. A quota consists in modifying the traded quantities, for example by limiting authoritatively the quantity imported of a particular good. The imposition of a customs duty – which increases the domestic price of a good – causes a decrease in the quantities that are exchanged (both the taxed good and the goods which are sold as a counterpart). Symmetrically, the imposition of an import quota causes a decrease in trade – in reality, exports as well as imports are reduced – and an increase in the price of the good thus protected (since it becomes scarcer).

• *The decrease in trade*: Let us take again the previous example in which only wheat and wine were traded internationally, and let us assume that, in the absence of protection (customs duties or quotas), the Brits import 10 pints of wine and export as a counterpart 15 pounds of wheat (with therefore a relative price of 1 against 1.5). At one point, the state imposes a quota in the form of a ban on importing more than 5 pints of wine. Since, on the international market, one exchanges 1 pint of wine against 1.5 pounds of wheat, exporters will have to reduce their exports: They shift from 15 pounds of wheat to 7.5 pounds of wheat.

We have thus reached a conclusion that is very close to the previous one: It is equivalent to limit imports or to limit the corresponding exports. It is a logical consequence of the inseparability of the purchase and sale parts of a transaction. The lower an import quota is set, the more international exchanges are reduced, and the closer one gets to a situation of autarchy.

• *The change in relative prices*: If the State puts a limit on wine purchases – which is the same as a limit on sales of wheat – this means that, compared with the situation of free exchange, there is less wine available in the country and more wheat (a part of the wheat that was exported to buy wine can no longer be exported and it must therefore be sold on the domestic market). Wine becomes relatively more rare (compared to wheat) and wheat relatively more abundant (compared to wine). It follows that the price of the rarer good is rising by simple application of the general theory of prices: the relative price of wine in terms of wheat increases (which also means that the relative price of wheat in terms of wine decreases). It comes closer to the relative price in isolation.

The imposition of a quota therefore causes a variation in the relative price very similar to the one that is directly introduced by a customs duty. In the case of a customs duty, one manipulates relative prices – by dissociating domestic prices from external prices – and, as a result, there are variations in traded quantities. In the case of quotas – also called 'quantitative restrictions on trade' – one manipulates traded quantities and, as a result, there is a change in relative prices.

The idea according to which it is equivalent to limit imports or exports seems simple when there are only two traded goods. But what can be said if there are large numbers of traded goods? If one limits the imported quantities of any good, one limits necessarily and simultaneously the quantities exported of some other goods. But it is generally impossible to know precisely which exports would take place if the existing quotas were removed. This idea may seem less obvious in a monetary economy. To make it simple, let assume a world with two countries, A and B, and let us assume that, initially, every individual holds the amount of money that he or she desires. If some people export goods from B to A, they get money in return, but they do not want to keep these cash-balances they do not need (since they had already an optimum amount of money). Symmetrically, some people in A need additional cash-balances since they had to pay for the imports from B. Thus, there is an excess supply of money in B and an excess demand in A. Money will shift from B to A thanks to imports by people in B from country A. If ever the state in country A decides to limit imports from B, there will be less money exchanged, but, once more, after a period of adjustment, the decrease in imports by country A will determine a decrease in its exports. It is nevertheless true that this adjustment of exports to imports is less immediate in a monetary economy than in a barter economy, but it exists, at more or less short term, because people do not want to increase or to decrease indefinitely their cash-balances.[3]

We can analyze the distribution effects of quotas in a way very similar to the one previously taken for customs duties. An import quota obviously benefits domestic producers of competing products because they have a 'captive market'.

The quota also incurs a cost for buyers because the goods they want are less abundant and more expensive. As for customs duties, quotas represent a transfer at the expense of buyers for the benefit of sellers (of goods protected from outside competition). There is creation of a monopoly position, made possible by the coercion imposed by the people of the state. It translates into the fact that there is an artificial – and compulsory – scarcity of the good in question. We know that, in such cases, the loss of some – in absolute terms – is greater than the gain of others.

But these effects are not the only ones. The scarcity of the protected good creates a "scarcity income" that may be shared among several partners. We have just seen that the producers of competing products were taking their share (in the form of larger domestic markets and higher prices for their products). But others can also benefit from this situation, especially the importers of the product in question and even, paradoxically enough in appearance, foreign producers of the good on which a quantitative limitation is imposed when it is imported in another country.[4] In fact, let us assume that the demand for the product on which there is an import quota be very slightly elastic: One is wanting it so much – compared to other goods – that the demand for this good is not decreasing very much when its price increases very much. The artificial scarcity on the market makes possible to sell the limited existing quantity of the imported good at a price significantly higher than the price that would result from a situation of free trade.

Let us use again the previous example: in a situation of freedom, Brit residents wish to buy 10 pints of wine against 15 pounds of wheat (with a relative price of 1/1.5) and let us imagine that, at this price, foreign wine exporters get a profit of 10%. In other words, for each pint of wine sold, they receive 0.1 pint of wine (or 0.15 pound of wheat) as a profit: The total value of their profit is therefore equal to 1 pint of wine or 1.5 pounds of wheat for 10 pints of wine sold.

Now suppose that the government, in Brit, prohibits imports of wine beyond 5 pints of wine. Suppose, too, that wine is so much desired in Brit that its domestic price shifts to 1 pint of wine = 3 pounds of wheat. For foreign producers, as it has been assumed, the production costs are such that one trades 1 pint of wine against 1.5 pounds of wheat (which gives them a profit of 10%). Therefore, those who sell wine in Brit will now get an additional profit of 1.5 pound of wheat per pint of sold wine. Of course, they sell less and they lose, therefore, the 10% profit they received on each pint of wine not sold. But for them this decrease is more than offset by the increase in price. In fact, each of the 5 pints which are still sold brings them an additional profit equal to 1.5 pound of wheat, so that they get a total profit of 7.5 pounds of wheat.

As we have seen previously, the theory of monopoly shows traditionally that the monopolist has an interest in making the quantities sold scarcer in order to raise prices, provided that the increase in unit prices brings in, in terms of total profit, more than what is lost from the decrease in the sold quantities (the profit being the product of the quantities sold by the unit profit). But the producer who would dream of being in such situation cannot generally get it when there is free trade.

State intervention then gives a unique opportunity to the foreign supplier (and/ or the intermediary, the importer) to limit access to a market, to make sold quantities scarce and to get prices higher than world market prices. The ability to take advantage of this monopoly situation – resulting itself from the state monopoly in legal coercion – depends on the responsiveness of demand to changes in prices, and therefore, on the existence of more or less close substitutes in the protectionist country. If, for instance, French people consider that French cars are goods very different from Japanese cars, quotas on imports of Japanese cars will encourage them to pay a high price for a Japanese car. In this case, it is not only the domestic producers who benefit from protection (because of wider sale opportunities and higher prices), but also (and even especially) foreign producers. If, on the other hand, the degree of substitutability is great, in the minds of potential users, between domestic products and foreign products subject to the quotas, domestic producers will benefit the most from protection. But consumers are always those who bear the cost of protection.

There is also another difference between customs duties and quotas. A customs duty, indeed, is a tax and therefore it brings revenues to the State. This is obviously not the case for a quota. But things are actually not so simple. In fact, a quota creates a situation of artificial scarcity where the access rights in a specific market are limited. The problem then arises of how one will assign these limited rights between various competing foreign producers and between different importers: Will the state bureaucrats allow the purchase of a product of such or such foreign brand, and promote such or such importer? The allocation of access rights to a market can obviously be made arbitrarily. But other procedures can be imagined. Thus, the state can sell these rights at an auction, in which cases it gets back a more or less important part of the previously studied monopoly gains so that the profit of foreign producers and importers is reduced.

But there are also other forms of redistribution of monopoly gains. An access right to a market has necessarily a market value in this environment of artificial scarcity, and a market for import rights will probably emerge. It is a legal market under the assumption we have considered: the one in which the state carries out an auction. But it may be – and it is often – illegal and hidden. The person who has the possibility to decide on the distribution of access rights – bureaucrat or politician – can monetise them, that is, request a bribe. In this case, the monopoly gain is not partially obtained by the public budget. It falls into the pockets of private individuals who benefit from a position of power in the public sphere. One can even imagine that, in some countries, the chance to obtain significant gains without particular productive efforts encourages potential beneficiaries to create and maintain quota systems. The protectionist arguments (which we study in Chapter 10) are then nothing but alibis for the personal confiscation of the resources of others.

Effective protection

For the time being we have implicitly reasoned as if international trade was related only to consumer goods. However, it may just as well concern intermediate goods that enter into production processes. Now, let us assume for instance that the Brits are importing wheat and selling tomatoes, the relative price between these two goods being equal to 1/1 (One exchanges 1 pound of wheat against 1 pound of tomatoes). In the absence of protection, this relative price is both the world price – therefore the price at which international exchanges of Brit take place – and the domestic price in Brit. Producers then buy wheat at this price, transform it into flour, and later cookies. Let us suppose finally that, with one pound of wheat – therefore a smaller quantity of flour – one produces a certain amount of cookies (for instance 1 pound) and that the price of 1 pound of cookies is equal to 2 pounds of tomatoes.

How is the price of cookies determined? At first glance, it corresponds to the cost of production, namely the price of the raw material – which is wheat – but also what may be called the set of added values resulting from the activity of the producers of cookies, in particular the cost of labour, the depreciation of machinery, the profit of producers.[5] The added value is therefore equal here to 1 pound of tomatoes per pound of cookies because one exchanges 1 pound of cookies against 2 pounds of tomatoes and one must buy 1 pound of wheat – worth 1 pound of tomatoes – to produce this pound of cookies.

In fact, it would be wrong to think that the selling price of the cookies is the simple result of a sum of costs of production (price of wheat, labour, etc.). The price is in fact determined by the market, that is, by the adjustment between supplies and demands. In the absence of protection, the market is global, meaning that there is a world price of a pound of cookies (assuming that one can define cookies as an homogenous good). Potential Brit producers of cookies look at the market for cookies, understand that, in order to sell and to make a profit, their production costs must be lower, or at most equal, to this world sale price. They will decide to produce cookies if they are able to compete with foreign producers. To this aim, they will eventually choose specific production techniques, taking into account, for instance, local specificities: if labour is abundant and cheap, they will choose techniques relatively labour-intensive and not capital-intensive, compared to what is probably decided in countries relatively better endowed in capital than in labour.

Therefore, even if all producers of cookies in the world do not use exactly the same production techniques, they all act so as to be competitive, so that their production costs are compatible with the prices prevailing on worldwide markets, as well for their raw materials (wheat) as for their final products (cookies). Ignoring the possible differences in transport costs, for reasons of simplification, we can then say that it is irrelevant for a producer in Brit to buy Brit or foreign wheat, insofar as there is a uniqueness of the market price. In the same way, it will not matter to consumers – in Brit or outside – whether to buy Brit or foreign cookies insofar as their prices will be the same.

Let us imagine now that, at some point of time, public authorities impose a customs duty with a rate equal to 50% on imports of wheat, meaning that it is necessary now to give 1.5 pounds of tomatoes to get 1 pound of wheat. This protection benefits Brit wheat producers since they can now get 1.5 pounds of tomatoes against 1 pound of wheat, due to the assumption of the uniqueness of prices on the market (and it is perhaps for this reason that the protection was introduced). But what happens from the point of view of the producers of cookies?

Apparently, nothing changes for them, since no one has introduced tariffs on cookies. But it means that the international prices still prevail for them. The raw material (wheat) which is needed to produce 1 pound of cookies is sold to them at a price of 1.5 pounds of tomatoes instead of 1 pound, whichever is the seller, either Brit or foreign. To be able to withstand foreign competition – at a price of 1/2 – they would therefore have to decrease the added value in such a way that it represents no more than 0.5 pound of tomatoes per pound of cookies produced: This would involve, for example, halving all remunerations (wages, profits, interests).

We can draw the following conclusions from this example:

- The benefit obtained by producers in a protected activity is necessarily obtained at the expense of others – consumers, but also other producers, not only those who lose their comparative advantage to export, but also those who use intermediate goods effectively protected in their production process;
- This example shows that we get a misconception of protectionist effects if we merely look at the apparent rate (the official rate). In the absence of additional information about production processes, it seems, in the example above, that a sector is protected – the wheat production sector – but the cookies production sector is neither protected nor penalised officially. But it has to bear a cost because of the protection of its suppliers, so that one can speak of negative protection (the producers of cookies are disadvantaged due to the protection of others and their earnings are lower than those they had when wheat was freely exchanged). In other words, to assess the protection (positive or negative) of a productive activity, it is not enough to consider the official rate of protection of the activity in question, but one must take into account the rate of protection of activities of which it is a client. In still other words, the degree of protection of an activity depends on the extent to which its added value is protected in comparison with the protection of its purchases of intermediate goods. Let us take again the above example and let us assume now that wheat production is not protected, but that the production of cookies is protected at an apparent 50% rate, so that the relative price of cookies after payment of customs duties is equal to 1 pound of cookies against 3 pounds of tomatoes (instead of 2). In reality, cookies producers enjoy a protection rate equal to 100% and not 50%: the apparent protection rate is equal to 50% and the effective rate to 100%. In fact, the producers buy 1 pound of wheat against 1 pound of tomatoes and the pound of cookies they get is sold at a price that allows payment for the factors of production – added value – at an amount equal to 2 pounds of tomatoes (instead of one). There is a doubling of value added, that is, a protection at a rate of 100%.

The example we have taken above was particularly simple, since we had assumed that producers of cookies bought only one intermediate good, wheat. It was therefore easy to realise that their protection was negative, when they had a zero rate of protection (no tariffs on cookies), but their suppliers had a protection rate equal to 50%. Real situations are obviously much more complex, so that one should ideally move up the chain of productive processes indefinitely to try to know the effective protection (positive or negative) of a product.[6] However, a number of studies have been made from input-output[7] tables to try to assess the effective tariff for a number of activities. The results are surprising. There is indeed a dispersion of effective rates of protection much larger than the dispersion of apparent rates of protection.

This result is normal because there are never apparent negative customs duties, whereas negative effective protection rates exist necessarily as soon as one puts tariffs on goods used into production processes (and any good can potentially be used not only as a final good but also as an intermediate good). The actual tariff structure therefore reflects negative protection levels that are obviously nonexistent in the official tariff structure. On another hand, calculations of effective protection rates show positive rates of protection that are sometimes considerably higher that what could be imagined by taking into consideration only official rates. Actual rates equal to 500% or 600% have been found. A producer who is protected in such a way can therefore stay on the national market, even though its production costs are in fact five to six times higher than those of foreign competitors. By allowing producers who have such a low productivity to remain on a market and by removing therefore the incentives to use the corresponding production factors in activities more productive but less protected, one ends up with a situation in which resources – human resources, capital, raw materials – are misused and wasted.

In our simplified example above, it was easy to see that the producer of cookies was suffering from negative protection. But in real situations where production structures and tariff structures are very complex, a producer is not easily aware of the rates of protection the enterprise enjoys or the rates at which it is suffering. The calculations we have mentioned are imperfect and obviously expensive. They can therefore not be carried out continuously and generally they do not have the degree of specificity sufficient for a particular producer to know its rate of protection (the degree of aggregation of the calculations is too high). Therefore, when the people of the state provide a protection to a particular activity, one can guess that it results in a negative protection for other producers who use – sometimes in a very indirect way – the protected goods in their production processes, but it is generally unclear who are these producers.

Notes

1 We have also seen in the first part of the book that competition, defined as the freedom to enter a market, has the great merit of encouraging innovation (of being a discovery process). Therefore, the freedom of trade, involving an extension of competition, also has this merit. One must consider this gain as an addition to what is called the 'exchange gain', that is, the gain due to specialization, which we studied previously.

2 Contrary to what is often believed, the strong growth of these countries is not 'pulled by exports'. It mainly comes from domestic sources, but the resources are not wasted by protectionism, which allows an important development of international trade, imports as well as exports.

3 One may find a more precise and more developed analysis of the role of money in such adjustment processes in our book, Salin (2016).

4 For example, at the end of the 1980s, the 'voluntary limitations' of exports of automobiles by the Japanese producers to the United States – following, in fact, agreements negotiated between American and Japanese governments – increased the profits of Japanese firms: 20% of its production exported by Honda in the United States brought 75% of its profits.

5 There are also, of course, other ingredients than wheat, for instance water, butter, etc. But to simplify the reasoning we are here concerned with a single raw material, wheat.

6 The producer of cookies uses pencils, the effective protection of which depends on the wood which itself depends on the protection of the transportation of wood, therefore of the protection of trucks and gas, etc.

7 That is, tables indicating the content of intermediate goods of each type of production. These tables give information of imperfect quality. It is impossible to know all the productive processes, the tables reflect an aggregation of activities in a number of sectors or branches arbitrarily delimited, it is unclear what would be the productive processes in the absence of protection, etc.

9 True and false barriers to trade

In the previous chapter we studied the usual protectionist measures – customs duties and quotas – which were specifically designed to *protect* a national activity from external competition. The protectionist effect is measured by the gap that is thereby introduced between, on the one hand, the relative price of two goods on the international market and, on the other hand, the relative price of these same goods on the domestic market. From this point of view, the protectionist intention does not matter much. As far as it causes a difference in relative prices between the inside and the outside, a measure of economic policy has a protectionist effect. The effects of such measures are the ones we have studied: changes in the structure of production, compulsory transfers, loss of well-being for some people.

We must therefore extend the study of protectionism to all situations in which a measure of economic policy translates into a difference in relative prices between the foreign market and the internal market, whether the protectionist effect has been desired or not.[1]

Tax policy

The protectionist effects of a tax policy – apart from customs duties, already studied – are not necessarily what one can imagine spontaneously. To analyze them, we will consider a simplified framework by assuming that there are only two countries in the world, Brit and Gaul.

Non-discriminatory taxes: Let us imagine that there is the same general tax in both countries, such as a tax on value added (VAT). As its name suggests, this tax is levied on an economic activity as a percentage of value created at each stage of the production process. It follows that any market price being a sum of added values, the tax that will have been levied in total, on a final good, after the various stages of its production, will be proportional to the sale price of this good. Now, let us suppose that a VAT – which did not exist previously – is suddenly created in each country and that its rate for all activities is 20% in Brit and 10% in Gaul. People generally think that this difference in rates between the two countries is unacceptable and that therefore some compensation has to be found for competition to be fair. In fact, they say, Brit producers are 'disadvantaged' in international trade, while Gaul producers are 'favoured'; or, to use the usual terminology, Brit producers are thus made less competitive than their competitors from Gaul. In other words, Brit producers would suffer a negative protection, while Gaul producers would benefit from a positive protection, due to the rising costs of their Brit competitors. And it is precisely because one believes that producers in the countries where VAT is the highest suffer a 'loss of competitiveness' that it has generally been decided – wrongly, as we shall see – that the VAT should be refunded on exports and paid on imports. But let us suppose for the time being that, unlike this habit, exports are tax-included.

In fact, the idea according to which a VAT would create gaps in competitiveness between countries is incorrect. We saw already that the concept of a 'global competitiveness' of a country was meaningless. A particular producer is competitive in international trade because another producer is less competitive, but it is not possible that, for instance, *all* Brit producers be not competitive. What explains international trade is the set of *relative prices* and not the absolute monetary prices. Therefore, levying a tax at the same rate on all added values in a country does not change relative prices: If, for instance, 1 pound of wheat is exchanged for 1 pound of tomatoes and if a VAT of 20% on each of these goods is introduced, one will still exchange 1 pound of wheat against 1 pound of tomatoes. The only consequence of the introduction of this tax will be to reduce the remuneration of the factors of production, since the state will take, at each stage of production 20% of the value created.[2]

In the same way, a VAT of 10% levied on all goods in Gaul does not alter relative prices. Before the introduction of VAT, one exchanged one pound of wheat against one pound of tomatoes, both in Brit and Gaul. This relative price remains the same after the creation of the VAT.

If we now leave the assumption of a barter economy and we consider a monetary economy, it seems that a change in tax systems has an impact on monetary prices. Indeed, let us assume that there were the following prices before the creation of a VAT: 1 pound of wheat = £1 (currency of Brit) and 1 pound of wheat = G1 (currency of Gaul). The exchange rate between the two currencies is therefore normally equal to 1/1. If it was true that the creation of a VAT – 20% in Brit and 10% in Gaul – increased monetary prices in the same proportion[3] one would get 1 pound of wheat = £1.2 and 1 pound of wheat = G1.1. It is quite obvious that the previous exchange rate, 1/1, would no longer be an equilibrium rate. If there is a floating exchange rate regime between both currencies, the exchange rate of currency £ should depreciate by 10%. If the exchange rate is determined by monetary authorities there ought to be a devaluation of 10% of this same currency.

But is it certain that the monetary price will vary exactly in proportion to the new tax? If the tax appears suddenly and unpredictably, producers may not have another choice than to try to increase their sale price correspondingly. But their new sale price can be maintained only insofar as the quantity of money increases in the same proportion, namely 20% in Brit and 10% in Gaul. Indeed, as clearly shown in monetary theory, monetary prices depend basically on the quantity of money. Thus, in reality, it is insofar as the increase in the quantity of money would be 10% greater in Brit to what it would be in Gaul, that the exchange rate of the currency £ should depreciate by 10% and not because different VAT rates would have been established. Thus let us suppose now that the quantity of money remains constant in each country. This means that the prices of goods must, sooner or later, go back to their initial values, namely 1 pound of wheat = £1 (= 1 pound of tomatoes) and 1 pound of wheat = G1 (= 1 pound of tomatoes). If, as a result, producers must sell their products at the same price as before, while VAT has been created, this necessarily implies that they will have to shift the burden of this VAT onto the remuneration of the factors of production: Wages, profits, interests are reduced by 20% in Brit and 10% in Gaul. In this case, the exchange rates remain constant, as well as selling monetary prices or relative prices between products: In Brit, as in Gaul, one exchanges one pound of wheat against one pound of tomatoes and the conditions of international specialization are not changed compared to those that existed before the introduction of a VAT in each country.

Therefore, whatever assumptions are made about the evolution of money supplies and the exchange rate – therefore about monetary prices – it remains true that relative prices are not determined by VAT rates. It is therefore wrong to say that Brit producers are disadvantaged due to a higher VAT rate. *Differences in VAT rates between countries have no protectionist effect.* We can therefore mention some implications of this idea, even if they are not directly related to protectionism. First of all, there is no justification for refunding the VAT on exports and paying it on imports. Because of this practice – which is widespread – it can be said that international trade is not exactly identical to domestic trade: When doing an international exchange, one must bear specific administrative constraints (information costs, administrative requirements, longer delivery times, etc.). This differentiation can be considered as a protectionist effect (internal and external trade are not perfectly substitutable). But it must be clear that this effect is not the result of differences in tax rates. It is the consequence of the fact that it is thought necessary to 'offset' these differences in tax rates and to establish special procedures when an exchange is international. In this case, there is probably no protectionist intention, but an intellectual error does exist. This is all the more striking in that the practice of reimbursing the VAT on exports is universally practised.

Another important consequence can be drawn from the idea that the VAT does not affect relative prices: If one shifts from a system in which the VAT is refunded on exports to a system where it is not – as is often proposed for the European Union – there would be absolutely no need to harmonise the VAT rates in the different countries concerned.[4]

Discriminatory taxes: Let us introduce now the assumption according to which there are different VAT rates in the same country, for instance a VAT rate on cars equal to 30% and a VAT rate on artichokes equal to 10% in Brit (the normal rate of VAT being 20%), while the VAT rate remains 10% in the other country, Gaul. One might then be tempted to say that producers of artichokes are protected, while car producers are disadvantaged (they get a negative protection). In reality, there is here an excessive extension of the concept of protection.

Let us consider first the case where the VAT is refunded on exports so that the tax system of a country is isolated compared to the rest of the world. The result is obviously that it matters little, from the point of view of international trade, that there is a differentiation of VAT rates within Brit: exports are made 'tax excluded'.

Now, let us consider the case where the VAT is not refunded on exports. Because of competition, relative prices within Brit are identical to relative prices inside

Gaul (if one does not take into account possible differences in transport costs). In the example above, despite differences in VAT rates, the relative price between cars and artichokes is the same in both countries. This necessarily implies that the VAT rate – which is higher on cars in Brit – be borne in reality by the factors of production who thus receive lower incomes (so that it may possibly result in an inability to compete efficiently with foreign producers). Symmetrically, the lower rate on artichokes implies that factors of production receive higher remunerations (or that they are able to compete with foreign producers, whereas they would not be competitive if they had to bear the normal rate).

Therefore, one might be tempted to say – at least in the case where there is no refund of the VAT on exports – that the differentiation of VAT rates within a country promotes (relatively) certain producers and disadvantages others, and therefore it could be analyzed as a measure with a protectionist purpose. However, this conclusion is inaccurate. Protectionism creates a gap between the relative price of both products within the country and the relative price of these products outside, which is not the case in the situation we just described, since the relative price between cars and artichokes is the same in Brit and outside. In reality, the differentiation of VAT rates discriminates against the producers of cars in comparison with the producers of other products, whether these producers are domestic or foreign. Symmetrically it encourages producers of artichokes, whether they are domestic or foreign. Therefore, there is no protection for domestic producers against foreign producers. A tax such as the VAT – whether it is differentiated according to the products or not, whether it is refunded on exports or not – has no protectionist effects, because it introduces no discrimination depending on whether the producer is foreign or not.

However, this is not necessarily the case with any or all taxes. Let us consider, for instance, the income tax. From a general point of view, it is the same to levy a tax under the form of a VAT – a tax based on added value and therefore on the remunerations that are the counterparts of added value – or under the form of an income tax, that is, a tax paid on the basis of distributed incomes. Let us take, for instance, the case of an individual whose work makes possible a creation of value equal to 100 over a period. It is the same for him if there is a 10% VAT – he gets 90 as an income (an added value of $100 - 10$ of VAT) – or if he gets an income equal to 100 and he has to pay an income tax equal to 10. But there is a difference between a VAT and an income tax: the territorial basis of these two taxes may be different. The VAT is levied on the basis of location of the different stages of the productive process, whether the owners of the corresponding incomes are located on the national territory or not. The income tax is normally levied on those who are residents on the national territory.

Let us therefore take the case of an individual located in country B and who has capital located in country A. This capital gives him a periodic return. If a VAT is created in country A, it affects the performance of this capital, the return of which is decreased. If there is an income tax, the return on capital is unaffected (but it may well have to bear an income tax in country B).

Let us suppose, however, that there are discriminations as regards the income tax, for instance because it is progressive (the tax rate is different depending on the level of income), and let us imagine the following hypothetical situation: There are two rates for the income tax in country A, 10% and 50%. There are also two categories of workers, those who have had an efficient training and those who have not. The first ones – whose remuneration is higher – are taxed at the rate of 50% and the latter at the rate of 10%. In addition, there is a single rate of the income tax, equal to 20%, in country B. Finally, two goods are produced, salads which require relatively few well-trained workers, and computers which require relatively many. Tax discrimination in country A relatively discourages workers trained versus untrained workers, which is not the case in country B.[5] The production of computers in country A is therefore relatively discouraged in comparison with the production of salads. However, the tax discrimination is applicable only to the producers of country A, and not to foreigners, unlike what was happening in the case where VAT rates were differentiated. There is a discrimination against domestic producers of computers and, symmetrically, a (relative) protection of domestic producers of salads. In this case, taxation has a protectionist effect. As we saw in Chapter 8, the protectionist effect enjoyed by some producers in a country is only the counterpart of the disadvantage (negative protection) that weighs on others.[6]

The statements we have just achieved can be interpreted as an extension of the strict concept of protectionism. The protectionist effect results from the fact that the concerned tax has two features that are also inherent to customs duties:

- The tax is differentiated (that is, there are different rates depending on the activities or persons);
- The tax discriminates between nationals and foreigners. In the case of customs duties, it hits products manufactured abroad, in the case of the progressive income tax it hits domestic residents and not foreigners.

Subsidies and regulations

The analysis of the protectionist effects of a policy of public transfers is obviously much easier than that of the effects of a tax policy. Let us take for instance the case of an industrial policy that grants public subsidies to specific firms or specific sectors of activity. As far as the beneficiaries are national and not foreign producers, it is typically a situation in which some producers enjoy a comparative advantage relative to their foreign competitors. They also benefit from a relative advantage over other domestic producers, since the resources they receive are necessarily collected from them. There are some differences, however, between a subsidy policy and a tariff policy:

- As we have seen, when the state is using customs duties, domestic relative prices become different from external relative prices. This is not the case with a policy of subsidies: They aim precisely at making domestic relative prices of some producers competitive with those of foreign producers. But insofar as subsidies allow producers to sell at prices below their cost of production, this policy helps to maintain production costs different from external relative prices. The protectionist effect is therefore identical to that of a policy directly protectionist (customs duties, for example): Resources – present or future – in a country are not used in the most efficient way, the structure of international trade is changed, the exchange gain is reduced, the gain of some producers is obtained at the expense of other producers or other individuals (the value of the gain of all beneficiaries being less than the value of the loss of others).

• When the state imposes customs duties, it receives the corresponding revenue. When it gives subsidies, it must instead find the necessary funding. We can consider that having recourse to subsidies has a relative advantage insofar as it allows better measurement of the cost of the privileges granted to some producers. But an accurate assessment of the two types of policies would require information on how subsidies are funded: tax shifts, distribution and effects of taxes, or of corresponding public borrowing. On the other hand, we have seen that, in certain circumstances, revenues from customs duties could be partially levied on foreigners, while subsidies are almost necessarily financed by the residents of the concerned country.

A subsidy policy and a direct protection policy can therefore be partly considered as substitutes for each other.

We may express the previous reasoning in a very general way by saying that the protectionist effect (positive or negative) is the result of the introduction by a state of a specific burden or a specific privilege involving a difference of treatment between citizens (or residents) of this state and foreigners. However, a specific burden can take the form of a regulation. We can point out that there is equivalence between a tax and a regulation. Indeed, let us assume for instance that a state wishes to build a road. It can build it itself and fund it by levying a tax. Or it may require a number of people – for example, those who benefit most directly from the road – to build it.

If a regulation imposes a particular cost for certain kinds of activities, relative prices are changed. However, by definition, a state can impose its regulations only to its residents: there is here an element of discrimination between nationals and foreigners that is characteristic of the protectionist effect. If, for instance, a state imposes specific safety or pollution standards for certain productions and if these standards have a *relatively* higher cost than is the case for standards abroad, the corresponding activities bear a negative protection (a relative disadvantage). Other activities of the country – which bear *relatively* less costly constraints – benefit on the contrary from a positive protection. As in other cases we met with previously, the protectionist intention does not necessarily exist. The protectionist effect is not less present, even if it is impossible to assess it.[7]

Notes

1 We saw previously that the actual protectionist effect could be different from the desired effect (in particular because of the existence of effective protection). In reverse, a measure can be taken for reasons other than protection, but it may have a protectionist effect.

Finally, it may happen that the protectionist effect is desired but not claimed as such, the measure being supposed to have a purpose other than protection.

2 The VAT should therefore be interpreted as a tax on the remuneration of factors of production, and not as a tax on consumption, as is implied by its name (tax on *value added*). It is only because one has introduced – wrongly – the practice of reimbursing the VAT on exports that the VAT *appears* as a tax on consumption.

3 This would imply in fact, as we explain below, that the money supply increases in the same proportion; otherwise, as monetary prices cannot increase, the monetary prices of the production factors would decrease, as noted above. But in all cases it is the actual remuneration of the factors of production that is diminished by the introduction of a VAT or the increase of the rate of an existing VAT.

4 We explain in detail the reasons for our hostility towards tax harmonisation in Europe in several texts, in particular in our book, Salin (2015)

5 Individuals are relatively less induced to get training in country A or, otherwise, they migrate from country A to country B.

6 It is strange that it is common – for public authorities as for public opinion – to call for the harmonization of VAT rates within the European Union and not for the harmonization of the progressive income taxes, while the first has no protectionist effects, unlike the second! This illustrates the fact that most public decisions are taken or discussed without any reference to economic theory.

7 In order to assess precisely the protectionist effect (positive or negative) on a given activity, one should, on the one hand, be able to assess the impact of the regulations on the production costs of this activity, but also the impact of all other regulations on all other activities in the country and abroad which affect relative costs of production and relative prices.

10 Protectionist arguments

According to what has been seen in the previous chapters, protectionism always means, regardless of the methods used, that some producers get a gain at the expense of other producers and of consumers. Furthermore, in accordance with the general theory of monopoly, the value of the resources lost by some is greater than the value of the resources thus obtained by others. The free trade argument seems thus unstoppable. However, one may say, protectionism exists and it is even widespread. Would this not prove that, despite its cost, it could meet some specific needs? Using evaluation criteria that we have not yet taken into account, one could perhaps find situations where the gain in terms of these criteria would more than compensate the loss of the benefits of free trade. We discuss in this chapter the most common arguments for protectionism.

The infant-industry argument

The infant-industry argument is probably the argument most used for protection. It is argued that the free trade theory would be 'static', in the sense that it would take into account the existing comparative advantages and not potential comparative advantages. In other words, it may well happen, according to the proponents of this argument, that an activity that appears not profitable at some point in a given country – when taking into account the prices prevailing on the world market and the internal production costs – could become profitable in the future. In fact, to obtain competitive prices, one should, for instance, reach a sufficient scale of production – which is not possible at the beginning of an activity – or benefit from a learning process that is necessarily time-consuming. Thus, it would be unfortunate to prevent the development of an activity that seems uneconomic in the short term, but that could become profitable within a few years. This argument seems to be convincing. However, it is not acceptable.

Let us look at things from the point of view of a producer who embarks on a new activity. He compares the present value of his current and future expenses and the present value of expected revenues.[1] He will start this activity if the expected profit – the difference between the sum of discounted expenditures and the sum of discounted revenues – seems to be sufficient. Moreover, it is not enough that the profit be positive for one to engage in an activity; it must be greater than the profit expected in other possible activities. It is no more sufficient, of course, that during a future period the revenues from this period be greater than the expenditures in this same period: it is necessary that this excess of revenues could compensate the losses of previous years. In other words, the profitability of an activity cannot be assessed by isolating arbitrarily the years in which revenues are greater than expenditures and not taking into account the years in which there has been a deficit.

It is reasoning of this kind that is implicitly done by those who support the infant-industry argument. They consider, in fact, that the profitability of an activity can be assessed by taking into account only the future periods in which – it is assumed – revenues will exceed expenditures. However, it is the very nature of an investment process that, in any activity, profitability may not be positive as soon as one begins the implementation of a project. The infant-industry argument therefore leads one to support artificially any project that is not cost-effective during a certain period. By artificially protecting an activity – for instance, by means of customs duties or subsidies – one changes the conditions of economic calculation and creates the feeling that an activity can be profitable, even though it should not be. Saying that an activity is profitable is saying that it generates over time more value than it destroys. Saying that an activity is not profitable is saying that it destroys over time more resources than it creates. Making believe that an activity is profitable, while it is not, means therefore wasting resources. One must not forget, indeed, that protection always has a cost: The additional gain obtained in the protected activity is the result of a transfer, meaning that other activities, other individuals, bear a cost (the absolute value of which is higher than the gain of those who are protected). Therefore, the greater apparent profitability of the protected infant industry necessarily corresponds to a lower profitability of other activities, whether or not they are infant industries. It may happen that the growth of these activities slow down or they may go bankrupt. A serious problem comes from the following fact: even though we are absolutely certain that this transfer effect between activities exists, we do not know in general which specific activities have to bear the cost of the protection afforded to others. It is pretty much impossible for someone who suffers a negative protection to identify the phenomenon and to connect it to the positive protection of others.

Insofar as the protection of infant industries leads to a waste of resources – creating, encouraging, and developing activities the costs of which are higher than the revenues that can be expected during their lives – the rate of growth of a national economy where such policies are generally used can be widely affected. It could even become zero or negative in inducing transfers of resources from profitable activities towards activities that are not. This phenomenon probably explains the low growth of many poor countries in which important protectionist policies are implemented, which are mainly justified by the infant-industry argument. This was the case, in particular, in many Latin American countries until fairly recent times: under the impulse of an economic doctrine essentially spread by Raoul Prebisch and the UN Economic Commission for Latin America (CEPAL), these countries have adopted economic policies based on 'import substitution': Wanting to produce inside what could be better produced outside and could be obtained thanks to international trade, the governments of these countries have caused a misallocation of resources and weak growth.

An additional consequence of the infant-industry argument consists in substituting the judgment of politicians or bureaucrats for that of the entrepreneur. Indeed, when an entrepreneur considers that it is desirable to launch an activity, in the absence of any protection, he or she takes into account all the information available and, in particular, some which are specific to him or her and which concern the ways in which the production process will be organized: techniques, modes of human relations, marketing policy, and so on. All this very diverse and complex knowledge is essential to the development of a firm. But it is only very partially communicable. The people who decide a policy for the protection of infant industries have absolutely no ability to know all the entrepreneurial projects that develop at any time in all branches of production. They have absolutely no means to decide which activities should be assisted by a protectionist policy. Their decision criteria cannot be related to expected rates of return of different projects. They use very different criteria: for example, the prejudices they may have in favour of certain activities, political pressures they get, and other incentives. For the decisions of entrepreneurs who are relatively well informed and responsible (since they bear themselves the consequences of their actions), one thus substitutes the decisions of politicians and bureaucrats who are ill-informed and not responsible (since they cannot be penalised for their bad choices and one cannot determine which activities were prevented from developing because others have benefited from protectionist privileges).

'Priority' and 'strategic' national activities

The protectionist argument according to which certain national activities are priority activities and must be protected is in fact very close to the infant-industry argument. Although it implicitly recognises the cost of protection, it considers that compensating gains must be taken into account. Of course, it is impossible to define rigorously what is a priority activity, and this is why this argument is used by those who have an interest (personal or otherwise) in trying to obtain the protection in question. As it is impossible to define this concept and to give a list of priority activities, let us take some examples about which the argument is frequently raised.

For example, one says that it is a national interest to protect activities in which technological innovation is important because there are 'technological spillovers' which other activities can enjoy. However, as is the case for all other resources, the resources which are used for technological innovation are scarce, whether human or material resources. The economic problem is thus mainly to make the best possible use of them. Let us imagine, for instance, that people are encouraged to move resources towards a certain sector A which enjoys a special protection under the pretext that innovations will eventually be useful in activities B, C, or D. If, truly, technological innovations are profitable in these activities, the corresponding resources will be requested and paid in a satisfactory way in the absence of any protection. But by directing resources to sector A through protection, one makes them unavailable for other sectors. The argument that stresses the potential technological impact of the protection granted to sector A is therefore unacceptable.

It is also often said that certain activities are 'essential' for the survival of a country or that they have a 'strategic' importance, so that they must be protected whatever the cost. One should prevent, for instance in the event of a war, the inhabitants of the country from being deprived of certain commodities, because in that case imports would become impossible (and domestic production would have disappeared as a result of foreign competition). This argument is not without interest, but it is virtually impossible to assess it generally. In fact it depends on specific and unfamiliar circumstances: which kind of conflict should we have to face, which alliances will remain possible? In reality, it is a problem of decision in a situation of risk. If one wanted to avoid absolutely any risk, it would be necessary that the inhabitants of the country be able to produce everything that is necessary, assuming that one can define 'what is necessary'. And one should also take into account the possibility that there would be a domestic revolution or an internal secession: At the limit, an absolute safety is achieved when each individual produces everything which he or she needs.

It is true that one takes a risk when one must resort to someone else to satisfy a need. But the gain brought by the development of trade would not have been possible if one had not accepted some risk. The 'strategic activity' argument is, from this point of view, an argument for turning down exchange.

There cannot be any objective test of what is 'essential' or 'strategic'. By accepting this protectionist argument, one thus takes the risk of lengthening indefinitely the list of what must be produced by a country without having recourse to imports, or even – why not? -what needs to be produced by a region, a town, a village, a district without resorting to the 'outside'. Because of its vagueness, the strategic argument for protection may thus be nothing more than an alibi to obtain special privileges: whether they are producing cars, phones, computers, or anything else, many producers may argue that their activity has a key strategic role.

Protection against dumping

One of the most frequently advanced arguments for protectionism is to say that some foreign producers or certain foreign countries practice dumping, which means that they sell their products at prices exceptionally low, so as to seize a market outside of their own national market. One should then protect domestic producers against this 'unfair competition'. At the limit, it is said, a foreign producer may decide such a low price policy in order to permanently eliminate the producers in the country concerned, with the intent of raising prices up to a normal level after having thus seized the market. For the time being, we will only deal with the case where producers have a policy of dumping on their own account. We will later see the case where this dumping policy is practised by the authorities of a country and not by a particular firm. But let us first define dumping.

Definition of dumping and examples: To evaluate the relevance of this protectionist argument, it is first necessary to get a precise definition of dumping. Dumping can be defined very simply as a situation of price differentiation: There is dumping when a producer asks a different price for the same product according to the market segment he addresses.

This practice is common in many activities and it results simply from the commercial strategy of entrepreneurs, eager to maximise their profits: The differentiation of prices makes possible to reach various clienteles. Thus, in the field of air transportation, there are normal fares and a number of lower rates. The latter ones apply specifically to categories of customers who would perhaps not travel if they had to bear the normal fare and who are willing to accept a certain number of constraints in return (fixed dates, minimum length of stay, prohibited stops along the way, etc.). Air transport activities would be uneconomic if everyone enjoyed the lowest fares. Symmetrically, if there were only normal fares, it would probably lead to a situation in which only partly empty planes would fly: It is not very costly for an airline to carry additional passengers, and the promotional rates therefore bring a profit.

Similarly, when a cinema offers lower prices to students on weekdays, it practises a policy of price differentiation. One is assuming that the resource potential of this type of clientele is limited, but that it has a greater availability of time, so that the owners of the cinema can thus maximise their receipts by getting a better filling of the room. In more technical terms, it can be said that price differentiation – dumping[2] – occurs when a producer has the ability to 'segment' his market between categories of buyers whose demands have different price elasticities: one will offer a lower price to those who are more sensitive to price.

Dumping by a foreign firm: It is perfectly rational for producers to do such a policy and it benefits consumers, since it allows them to obtain a greater differentiation of prices and services, and therefore a greater chance to meet their own needs. It is therefore difficult to consider that price differentiation is reprehensible. Why, then, should one turn down the dumping of foreign firms? Indeed, if price differentiation was harmful, one should repress it to the same degree when it is practised by a 'national' firm as one does when it is done by a 'foreign' firm. One should therefore, for example, prohibit airline special rates or lower prices for students in cinemas; or even levy special compensatory taxes – similar to anti-dumping customs duties – in order to protect producers who do not practice price differentiation (perhaps because they have a bad commercial policy). And if price differentiation is not reprehensible – which is indeed the case – why should one punish it when practiced by producers who are located in a foreign territory? The traditional justification of 'anti-dumping customs duties' may therefore be an alibi for those who ask for this protection and those who give it.

Doing dumping is less easy than one generally thinks. It presupposes that one can actually segment markets. This was the case in the examples above, since it is not possible for a student to resell his seat in a cinema at a price closer to the normal price or for the owner of a low-fare air ticket to remove the constraints that are tied up with it. There is in fact a strong personalization of the product in these cases. But it is much more doubtful that it is possible to do the same with goods which are fungible, or readily transmissible. Thus, if a Japanese producer of cars offers particularly low prices in France so as to destroy the French car industry, he would have to face the risk that his cars be re-exported to Germany, Italy, or even . . . Japan, if the price difference between the regular price and the dumping price was greater than transport costs. The Japanese producer would thus be supplanted in many countries by French importers of Japanese cars who would re-export them and who would receive, instead of him, a very great part of the profits from the sale of cars. That is to say that a policy of price differentiation easily finds its limits and that dumping is less generally used than it is claimed.

Similar difficulties exist with the concept of 'predatory dumping': selling at a loss on the market of a country so as to cause the bankruptcy of the producers of this country, to replace them later and to enjoy 'monopoly profits'. Let us imagine, for instance, that a car producer A, located in a country called Nippo, is considering doing such a policy in another country, called Gaul. According to the information available to him, he calculates as likely that he can bring the industry of Gaul to bankruptcy in thirty months by supporting a loss equal to N. For this 'game' to be worthwhile, the present discounted value of profits he will get later, after having taken hold of this car market, must be at least equal to N. These are the caveats:

- If it is truly possible to do so, one wonders why other producers wouldn't have done so. In particular, one could very well imagine that one of the producers of cars of Gaul could decide such a policy: if, for example, there are two producers in Gaul, one of them could seek to eliminate the other so as to be master of the national market. If other producers from Nippo, apart from producer A, do not engage in this policy, it may be because the risk is too big for the game to be worthwhile; or that those other producers are not efficient enough to take such risks.

- When a producer plans to embark on an action of 'predatory dumping', it engages in the following reasoning: 'If we succeed in ruining the car industry of Gaul, we cannot be certain that we can have a monopoly and fix our selling price at a level that would be the most profitable for us. Indeed, there are other car producers in the world and each of them will perhaps try to take advantage of the opportunity we will have created by ruining the producers of Gaul. We therefore have the risk that we bear the loss N for others to get a profit. Is this risk worthwhile?'. In most cases, the answer is probably negative, the more so, indeed, that the degree of risk of this action is important. How much time will it take to ruin the car industry of Gaul, what will be the actual amount of the loss N, is there a risk of retaliation from the government of Gaul? For the 'predatory dumping' to exist, it would be both necessary that the level of risk be low and that the 'predatory industry' meet virtually no competition. This means that 'predatory dumping' is probably nothing more than a myth, but a myth that it is convenient for underperforming producers to call up, so as to obtain protectionist measures from their government.

Generally, a market economy – which is therefore an innovation economy – is characterised by the fact that corporate strategies collide continually one with the other and they include, in particular, the elimination of competitors. Each producer tries to maximise his long term profit, the extension of his market being a component of this strategy. In a competitive economy, the longterm selection is in favour of the most successful firms, that is, those that produce the best products at the lowest cost. And this selection necessarily implies the disappearance of less successful firms. It is absurd to say that the first ones are doing 'predatory dumping' and, even more, that they create an 'unfair competition'. It would certainly not come to the minds of anyone to interpret in such a way a situation in which competition takes place between two firms of the same country. One would only recognise the merits of one and the flaws of the other. It is therefore not logical to think otherwise when it happens that the two concerned producers are located on different national territories.

The following is actually happening. It is relatively difficult – but not completely impossible – for an inefficient firm to ask its government to protect it (thanks to subsidies, quotas, regulatory measures, etc.) against the alleged 'unfair competition' from another producer of the same country, because the latter would do symmetric pressures on its government against this specific protection. On another hand, if this other producer is located in another national territory, the less efficient producer can seek the protection of its government, for example under the pretext that there is 'predatory dumping', without the more efficient producer being able to exert a countervailing pressure on this same government.

Economic progress has been historically possible, particularly in the Western world, because governments did not generally agree to protect inefficient firms against competition from more efficient firms. Had they done so, we would have had stagnant economies for centuries. We would use candlelight, we would use carts pulled by horses, and we wouldn't get enough care for our children. Economic nationalism, consisting of using a diametrically opposite reasoning when competition takes place between firms located in different territories and when it concerns firms with the same nationality, therefore necessarily slows down economic growth.

In other words, the idea according to which protectionism would be justified to prevent the 'dumping' of some firms actually means using coercion – since protection is imposed by the state – to give a monopoly position to some firms under the pretext of avoiding future monopolistic positions (from foreign firms) which are in fact generally fictitious.

We can finally point out that it is strange to criticise producers for doing price differentiation – which they do not necessarily do or which they do for reasons of productive efficiency – while one does not think of blaming governments for doing protectionist policies. Yet these policies are obviously measures of price differentiation.

Dumping decided by a 'country': We assumed above that price differentiation resulted from the explicit decisions of the exporting firm, which seeks to maximise its profit. But price differentiation may result from a state intervention. This is the case if, for example, a state subsidises a specific export.[3] It follows that the product thus subsidised enjoys a comparative advantage that would not be justified by its 'natural' conditions of production. There is actually a price differentiation, depending on whether the product is sold in the national or foreign market, even though this differentiation does not result from the decisions taken by the firm that produces this commodity.

To which extent may a countervailing protectionism in the importing country be then justified so as to avoid the competitive advantage thus obtained by the foreign producer? The argument is actually not much different from the one we have already used. Indeed, one can imagine that a state seeks to exercise 'predatory dumping' by providing subsidies to some exports. But, from the point of view of the importing country, it matters little that the loss corresponding to the price differentiation is borne by a foreign producer or by a foreign state. The fact that the relative price of a good is thus decreased for the inhabitants of the importing country is in any case a gain for them: foreign taxpayers subsidise them by reducing the price of the commodity they import. Why should one not enjoy it, why should one try to cancel this gain by compensating customs duties? To be sure, even though the producers of this subsidised commodity in the importing country suffer a loss, the fact remains that, overall, the inhabitants of the importing country receive an external grant. The economic calculation is not quite of the same nature in this assumption and in the assumption of a differentiation of price decided by the producing firm. In the latter case – the one we have previously studied – the firm has an interest in comparing the current cost of differentiation and the gain that it can hope for in the future. If price differentiation is the result of a state intervention (subsidy), there are two decision centers possibly aiming at different targets. It is likely, for instance, that politicians are not looking at obtaining a maximum profit in the long term for the concerned exporting firms, but that they simply seek political benefits in the short term by providing a specific privilege to these firms.

But one can also say that this specific state intervention is part of the set of production conditions that determine comparative advantages and there is no particular reason to isolate it and to compensate for it, while there are other causes of differentiation of production costs between the two countries, many of which are perhaps of state origin. Thus, if an activity must bear a specific regulation in a country, if there are specific taxes or if a state is financing the training of some employees, all comparative advantages are changed. However, it is impossible to calculate what the relative prices would be if the state did not intervene and, therefore, to try to compensate, by customs duties in the importing country, the effects on relative prices of all state interventions abroad. These interventions certainly represent causes of differentiation of productive structures, from which one must try to draw, thanks to international trade, any possible advantage.

It is finally necessary to challenge an idea that is often expressed, and which consists, for instance, in saying that low-wage countries are doing dumping, because their producers are able to supply certain commodities at very low prices. But this is a wrong use of the word 'dumping' since, as we have seen, there is dumping when there is price differentiation, which is not the case. But beyond the misuse of the term, one must also challenge the justification thus given to protectionism. In fact, we have already seen that trade is beneficial to both parties insofar as they do not produce under the same conditions. If labour productivity – and therefore real wages – are low in a country, it is in everyone's interest that this country be specialised in productions requiring relatively labour-intensive techniques, whereas its partners be specialised in productions requiring relatively more capital and advanced technology. Let us then push to its extreme limit the argument according to which one should protect oneself from the competition of a country which would have a relative advantage due to the existence of low wages. Any relative advantage should then be considered as unacceptable and should result in some compensating protectionism, until international trade would become impossible. And why would the argument be valid for relations between countries and not relations between regions? It would therefore be necessary to protect producers of a region against competition from producers in other regions benefiting from specific advantages. And why not, then, protect towns and villages until, finally, one would prohibit all exchanges between people and therefore all economic progress?

Balance of payments equilibrium

Protectionism is often put forward or used as a policy aiming at 'external equilibrium': the elimination of what is called a 'balance of payments deficit'. To assess this argument, it is necessary to understand what the balance of payments is. The balance of payments of a country is an account that traces all transactions during a period between a country and the rest of the world. One can distinguish three main components of the balance of payments, corresponding to the three main categories of traded goods: the account of commodities and services, generally called the trade balance, the account of financial assets (or capital balance), and the monetary account. One says that there is a 'balance of payments deficit' if the country is a net seller of money and therefore a net buyer of commodities and/or financial assets. The analysis of the balance of payments should be considered a simple application of the general theory of exchange, which we have presented in Chapter 7.[4] As we do know, in any transaction there is always a sale part and a purchase part, which cannot be separated one from the other. An individual or a group of individuals – for example, those who constitute a country – buy because they sell, they sell because they buy. This simple proposal leads to another proposal concerning the balance of payments: one cannot change a part of a transaction – the sale or the purchase part – without changing the other part. And it is this statement that had led us to conclude, in Chapter 8, that protecting imports meant simultaneously protecting exports. Then we considered only the exchange of commodities against other commodities, while we are now introducing the possibility of exchanging financial assets or currencies.[5] It is therefore wrong to think that one can, for example, decrease imports of commodities without simultaneously reducing exports of commodities or without changing another item of the balance of payments (i.e. decreasing the sales of financial assets and/or money or increasing the purchases of these goods).

Let us suppose first, to simplify the reasoning, that money does not exist, but that there are financial assets (bonds, shares, various claims). International flows of financial assets are the counterpart of commodity flows. If, for example, there is a trade deficit – that is, sales of commodities are lower than purchases – there must be a surplus in the balance of financial assets (asset sales are greater than purchases). The country therefore sells financial assets against goods. Now, financial assets represent future goods because they are rights on future resources. The trade deficit is therefore a purchase of present goods against a sale of future goods. This exchange takes place when the appreciation of time – usually called 'time preferences' – is different in the country and in the rest of the world: The inhabitants of the country which has a trade deficit give relatively more value to the present, they promise to give up resources in the future in order to be able to get resources immediately. If, for example, there are significant opportunities of investment in a country and a rate of savings relatively low (compared to the rest of the world), it will be quite normal that this country has a trade deficit and, at the same time, a surplus in its balance of financial assets. Policies to reduce the trade deficit cannot succeed, insofar as they do not affect the time preferences, which explain the structure of the balance of payments. Thus, customs duties or quotas on imports or subsidies on exports have strictly no effects on the trade deficit. By reducing imports, one also decreases exports, without modifying the choices between the present and the future, which involve an exchange of present goods (trade deficit) against future goods (financial assets). The intellectual error committed by all those who believe that one can 'fix' a trade deficit by modifying imports (or exports) stems from the fact that they forget that a transaction always has two sides: a purchase side and a sale side. Modifying one is necessarily modifying the other.

Now, let us assume that currencies exist and that they are traded internationally. It may be that the inhabitants of a country are neither buyers nor sellers of currency over a period, if a currency is used momentarily as an intermediary in trade. The balance of the trade balance then corresponds, as above, to the balance of the balance of financial assets (and the balance of the monetary balance is equal to zero). But let us suppose that several countries are under a regime of fixed exchange rates – meaning that different currencies can be considered as being equivalent – and money creation is abundant in a country. Individuals in this country having more money cash-balances than they wish, money tends to leave this country and there is what is called, according to a questionable terminology, a 'balance of payments deficit': the sales of currency have as a counterpart, for instance, purchases of commodities. Now, the problem is not an (external) balance of payments problem, but an (internal) problem of excess money creation. This is not an 'excess', more or less inexplicable, of purchases of commodities causing a trade deficit and, therefore, a 'balance of payments deficit' (sales of money). It is an excess of money creation that causes outflows of money and, as a counterpart, inflows of commodities. It is not by trying to make purchases of commodities scarcer that one can put an end to excess money creation.

Therefore, policies that try to influence the trade balance and to remove a trade deficit cannot succeed insofar as they do not alter the causes of this deficit, that is, the excess of money creation or preferences for the present. Therefore, the balance of payments argument in favour of protectionism is not acceptable.

We may consider that so-called exchange controls – which are in fact controls of the international flows of money – constitute a modality of protectionism, at least if one accepts a broad concept of protectionism. Exchange controls can be defined as a policy to prohibit, to limit or to subject to authorization all international transactions – or parts of them – made by the residents of a country. Protectionism is often defined as a set of measures to limit or prohibit purchases of foreign goods. Insofar as exchange controls aim at affecting transactions, whether they concern commodities, assets or currencies, we can consider them as a simple extension of the traditional concept of protectionism. And it can also be analyzed exactly in the same way. Let us suppose for instance that there are restrictions on the international exchanges of financial assets in a country. Insofar as these exchanges are necessary counterparts of flows of commodities or currencies, these latter are necessarily affected.

Let us take, for instance, the case in which purchases (imports) of financial assets have as a counterpart sales (exports) of commodities. If one restricts purchases of foreign assets, one reduces necessarily and at the same time sales of commodities. Generally speaking, it is impossible to influence one item of the balance of payments without influencing another one. But one does not generally have the means to know which items are thus affected, because one never knows the reasons why this or that transaction takes place. More generally, and contrary to common opinion, we can say that *there can never be a balance of payments problem*. Therefore, protectionism and exchange controls cannot be justified by the necessity to influence a balance of payments.

Protecting employment

The argument concerning the protection of employment can have two different aspects:

- A general aspect consists in emphasizing that production is greater – and therefore jobs are more numerous – the more a country is selling (or the less it buys);
- A sectoral argument consists in saying that foreign competition may limit the production of some specific sectors and perhaps even lead them to bankruptcy, which would cause unemployment.

Let us consider first the sectoral argument. It consists in saying that, given the existing real wage rates, a sector for which a special protection is claimed is not 'competitive'. Now, protection implies, as we have seen, that one is moving resources to the protected activity. It may thus happen that it absorbs resources that are worth more than what it produces.

The aim of any individual – entrepreneur or head of a family – is to make the best use of the resources available to him or her. Thus, an entrepreneur will not seek to maximise the number of employees, but to induce them to work as well as possible. The idea of 'protecting jobs' in a sector or a particular activity goes exactly in the opposite direction. And if it was applied widely in all sectors, it is economic progress – which is enjoyed by everyone – which would be affected. By protecting an activity, under the pretext of protecting employment, one destroys the price signals that would, little by little, induce this sector of activity to adapt to circumstances and to the needs of consumers. In the absence of protection, entrepreneurs would adopt different techniques to compete with foreign producers; some employees may leave the noncompetitive activities to go to other, more competitive, ones. This gradual adaptation to the evolution of the environment is an integral part of economic life. Everyone has the responsibility to try to forecast the future, and from this point of view, the evolution of prices is an irreplaceable guide. Although forecasting can never be perfect, one certainly does not improve it by hiding price signals.

Now, when protection has been obtained, it becomes increasingly difficult to delete it. Instead of the gradual adaptation that would have occurred in a situation of free trade, one is faced with the risk of a deep shock, when an activity has been protected for a long time and one mentions submitting it to external competition. The failure to adjust productive structures to the outside world – caused by protection – may create significant unemployment in the concerned sector, at least momentarily. And this risk is then invoked to maintain or even strengthen protection.

The global argument according to which protection helps to maintain a high level of employment is roughly as follows: If one protects domestic producers against outside competition, one will limit imports and, therefore, generate a trade surplus (or, at least, limit the trade deficit). The more important are exports compared to imports, the stronger is the demand for domestic production; and the more important this production is, the higher is the level of employment as a result.

There are therefore two main statements in this traditional argument:

- a relationship between protectionism and the trade balance
- a relationship between the trade balance and employment.

Unhappily, these two parts of the traditional argument are wrong. We already know, indeed, that it is an illusion to believe that, by creating obstacles to imports, one obtains a decrease in the trade deficit or the appearance of a surplus. Therefore, it is not necessary to give more attention to this part of the argument.

By destroying a part of the chain of reasoning, one obviously destroys all this reasoning, and this first statement ought to be considered as sufficient to reject the global employment argument. But we could explain also why the second part of the reasoning is also incorrect. We will not do this in the limited context of the present text, since it would require a long discussion of macroeconomic theory. However, one may simply ask the following question: How is it possible that domestic producers do not produce more – and, therefore, do not increase employment – although world markets exist so that they could export much more? Why should it be necessary, in order to increase economic activity, to diminish imports authoritatively, although the possibility to export is always open? This means necessarily that, if producers do not produce more, if employment is not higher, it is for reasons – probably internal – which have nothing to do with trade. To solve the unemployment problem one should suppress its internal causes (for instance, an excess of regulations and taxes). These causes can certainly not be suppressed by limiting imports. We also know that an economy where some sectors are protected from outside competition is less efficient than a free trade economy. How could it be then possible to offer as high wages – to a larger number of people – in a protected economy as in a free trade economy? It is clear that the employment argument for protectionism stumbles on a logical inconsistency.

Taxes and 'optimum' customs duties

Customs duties are taxes and, as such, they can play the main role of all taxes, namely transferring resources to the public power. This tax role is not negligible in some countries where the tax collection system is embryonic and expensive relative to its performance. The use of customs duties seems therefore relatively justified. One should, however, make a cost-benefit analysis and compare this financing solution to other possible solutions:

- Levying customs duties implies administrative costs, not only for the government but for citizens. It would be appropriate to compare them with the administrative cost of collecting other taxes.
- The burden actually borne by the population of a country because of protection can be high (despecialisation effect) and it is generally not known accurately. This phenomenon of ignorance and the apparently painless nature of protection may lead to giving added weight to customs duties in a tax system, even though their actual costs for citizens would be higher than those of other types of taxes.
- In any case, one should separate the protectionist effect from the monetary price effect. The protectionist effect corresponds to the distortions in relative prices (either between different goods or between imports and exports) introduced by customs duties, while the absolute price effect consists only in a change of the level of monetary prices for all goods.

Now, let us assume that the government of a country suddenly imposes tariffs at a uniform rate – 10%, for example – on all imports (so that transactions 'imported goods against exported goods' are taxed at 10%, since we know that a tax cannot be borne only by one part of a transaction) and that, as a compensation, it revalues its currency by 10%. This means that domestic prices are increased by 10% when there are international transactions because of customs duties, and they are simultaneously reduced by 10% as a result of the revaluation. The conditions of competition between this country and the rest of the world are therefore not changed (since relative prices remain the same), but international transactions are taxed compared to domestic transactions. Therefore, there is no protectionist effect, in the sense that no activity is privileged compared to others, but there is a tax levy on international transactions.

But let us go back now to the hypothesis in which customs duties are not identical for all goods, but differentiated according to goods, which leads to changes in relative prices, which are the expression of the protectionist phenomenon. We saw previously (Chapter 8) that the tax levy corresponding to the tariff was not necessarily paid by the inhabitants of the country that requires it, but that a part could be passed on to foreigners. It will be all the more important that the relative importance of the country – at least for traded goods – will be greater.

Let us take, first of all, the case of a very small country compared to the rest of the world. Its protectionist policy will affect in a negligible way relative prices in the rest of the world, while domestic prices will be strongly affected. However, it is the gap between prices before customs duties and prices after customs tariff that allows one to appreciate the weight of customs taxes. In this case, therefore, almost all of the weight of the tax is borne by nationals under the form of a 'despecialisation' effect.

If, on the other hand, the relative size of the country compared to the rest of the world is large, its customs policy will result in a relatively large variation in relative prices in the rest of the world. One can then demonstrate that, in certain circumstances, the tax transfer thus imposed by the government on foreign economic agents can be larger than the cost of the protection that it imposes on its citizens. This is the so-called optimum tariff.[6]

The optimum tariff is then designed as a pure instrument of taxation. It is the expression of the monopoly power of the state. As noted earlier, in the traditional theory of monopoly the producer, who is supposed to know the demand curve, sets the price that gives the maximum benefit. The producer increases the price until the additional gain is just offset by the decrease in sales. But this theory of monopoly is here applied, as it should normally be, to the behaviour of public powers. Furthermore, because the state is able to impose price discrimination between inside and outside, it is its power to collect taxes from foreigners that is thus highlighted.

We saw previously that the loss due to the despecialisation effect was higher than the gain obtained by the state. The analysis of the optimum tariff is not in conflict with this idea. It is simply a special case in which the loss is specifically borne mainly by foreigners. But the total loss is always greater than the gain obtained by the protectionist state.

In addition, a few concluding remarks can be made about the optimum tariff:

• First of all, there is an asymmetry in the use of the optimum tariff. A small country has relatively fewer possibilities to be able to manipulate customs duties to retrieve a tax on foreigners. However, in our time, the small, poor countries are often relatively more protectionist than the major developed countries. Is it because their governments prefer that the tax be borne by their own citizens rather than by foreigners, or because protection corresponds to other aims than being a tax basis, those we already met or those we still have to examine?

• Looking for an optimum tariff would be possible if one had a perfect knowledge of the characteristics of supplies and demands for all goods and for all countries; and if, in addition, one had knowledge of the evolution of these characteristics over time. This is obviously not the case, so that the optimum tariff remains a theoretical possibility more than a practical one, if not an easy alibi.

- Finally, the government of a country can never pretend to be alone in manipulating rates of protection, and the reactions of other governments can threaten what was believed to be an optimal tariff structure. We are thus led to consider the so-called retaliation tariff.

Retaliation tariffs

As one of the numerous protectionist arguments, let us finally consider the so-called retaliation tariff. According to this argument a country should legitimately decide customs duties to answer to the barriers that other countries build against its exports. This argument is in fact very often used, for example, in the following form: 'It is true that the European Union is doing protectionist policies, but the United States and Japan are protectionist and therefore it is normal that the European Union also defends itself'.

The arguments we have made previously provide a first answer to this statement. We saw indeed that – except in extreme cases where there are reasons to believe that the tariff structure is optimal in the sense we have stated above – a customs duty is harmful first and mainly for the inhabitants of the protectionist country, and this is especially true when the country is small compared to the rest of the world (despecialisation effect). By imposing a retaliatory tariff, it is therefore harmful for itself first. In other words, it is not because others are doing silly things that one should also do silly things to take revenge on them. For instance, let us suppose that a stupid king in Gaul was punishing by fine or imprisonment the most efficient producers. The result would obviously be a lower efficiency of the economy, which would first affect the inhabitants of Gaul but which would also be detrimental to the inhabitants of other countries, because exchange gains would be reduced. Would it be justified that other monarchs do the same and punish the most efficient producers of Germania or Albion, on the pretext that it would be harmful for the inhabitants of Gaul? This reasoning would be absurd. However it is in fact the same one that is made when claiming protection under the pretext that others are protectionist.

This general answer being made, we can still consider a particular case, namely that where tariff retaliation could be considered as the answer of a country (Germania) to an optimum tariff imposed by another country (Gaul). By imposing a certain tariff structure, Gaul collects resources on the inhabitants of Germania. Unable to directly influence the public authorities of Gaul, the public authorities of Germania thus impose a tariff that is optimum, taking into account the existence of the customs tariff of Gaul. Germania thus gets back part of the tax paid to Gaul, perhaps with the hope that Gaul will waive a tariff policy which thus became less (or not at all) profitable. It may even happen that the simple prospect that Germania could impose a retaliatory tariff leads the State of Gaul to abandon its optimum tax project.

But another sequence of events is also possible: public authorities may engage in a tariff war, a retaliation tariff replying to another, until, possibly, any exchange disappears. All would be losers in this game in which everyone would have wanted to get the maximum, taking into account what had been previously done by the other. International trade having disappeared, the gains of trade also disappear, as well as the revenues of customs duties. It would be better, then, to use bargaining. We will discuss it in Chapter 12.

Notes

1 A discounted value – let us recall – consists in evaluating a future value in terms of current values. Let us call V^t the expected value of a variable – for example, a stream of income – in a future period t (the current year being year 1). The present value of V^t is equal to $V^t/(1 + r)^t$ where r is the rate of interest. In fact, 1+r represents the relative price of time: One can shift from the current period to the next period or vice versa by using this relative price. If, for example, the interest rate is equal to 10% per year, the current value of a claim which will be worth 110 next year is equal to 100. Indeed, it is the same to hold 100 today (which gives an income of 10% per annum) or to hold the promise of getting 110 next year: On the financial market one can sell this asset at a current price equal to 100.

2 It is usual to mention dumping when referring to the price policy of foreign producers. The mistrust that has developed about dumping in our time gives a negative meaning to this term. As regards the term 'price differentiation' it is considered as neutral. But the term 'dumping' should also be considered as neutral. It is the same reality.

3 We do not consider here the case, referred to in Chapter 8, in which subsidies at the same rate are granted to all exports, but the one in which there is a specific subsidy benefiting only one product or a limited number of products.

4 One may find a detailed analysis of the balance of payments in our book, Salin (2016)

5 In Chapter 8, we had introduced money, but mainly as a numéraire which can be used to label prices. We now consider it more explicitly as a good that can be desired for itself, because of the services it provides. Concerning the analysis of the roles of money, one may refer again to our book Salin (2016).

6 Of course, the optimum in question is a global optimum: for the country as a whole, the gain thus obtained from abroad is greater than the loss due to the despecialisation effect. But there are also distribution effects: the gain is in fact mainly obtained by the State and the situation of each citizen will thus depend on the use that the State will make of these resources. Now, it may happen that a given citizen loses much because of the despecialisation effect and that he or she earns little or nothing as a beneficiary of public services.

11 The role of political processes

The benefits of free trade are so obvious that one may naturally wonder why protectionism is so widespread. However, it follows necessarily from explicit decisions made by the 'people of the state' (politicians and bureaucrats), and therefore it is about their motivations that we have to wonder. Why do they introduce measures that are harmful for most citizens, as can be easily demonstrated?

Only two reasons can explain such a situation: protectionism is due to the fact that some people are pursuing their own interests (at the expense of the interests of others) or that they are ignorant (or both . . .). Ignorance does of course play its role, and just to be persuaded it is sufficient to notice how easily the infant-industry argument – which we have discussed in Chapter 10 – is widely accepted. But ignorance, either the one of those who decide, or the one of public opinion, plays only a secondary role. It mainly plays the role of inducing people to accept more easily decisions that are actually designed to protect special interests. It is this factor we will consider.

The game of interests

In very general terms we can say that protectionism is the expression of a political game among special interests that seek to use the monopoly of coercion of the state. Any political power is indeed specifically relying on certain categories of citizens who get its privileges. Protectionism is a way to provide them.

Let us take, for instance, a democratic society in which a particular 'clan' (political party, election coalition) needs a majority of votes to get power or to keep it. All the political game is to obtain the support of different categories of voters by taking into account their specific interests. On the one hand, votes are obtained in elections by granting privileges (in the form of subsidies, legislation, protection, etc.). On another hand, one is likely to lose power by having to make some citizens bear the weight of the corresponding measures: Indeed, nothing can be achieved for free, and if some citizens get state favours, there is also a set of citizens – the same or others – from whom the state needs to find the corresponding resources.

The problem that politicians have to solve is simple to express: how to maximise the probability of gains in an election by distributing favours, while minimizing the discontent of those who bear the actual cost of these measures?[1] From this point of view, it is preferable to give well-targeted and noticeable benefits, so that the beneficiaries are aware of what political power brings to them and, on the other hand, to make the corresponding levy as little visible as possible, as little painful as possible for voters.

To minimise the political risk due to the dissatisfaction of those who pay public measures, the people of the state can choose between two techniques:

- Getting taxes from a very small number of people who will obviously be hostile to them, but given that each voter has only one vote in modern democratic regimes, regardless of his or her tax contribution, the loss of votes in elections is limited;
- Asking payment from a very large number of people so that the introduction of a new measure in favour of a particular category of voters – for example, entrepreneurs and employees of a specific branch of activity – does result in a practically negligible increase in the burden borne by others. The political effect is enhanced if one finds a way to hide from voters that they are those who actually pay the measure in question.

Thus, each particular privilege granted by the people of the state gives them votes, without losing a lot. But as privileges accumulate, the tax burden – directly or indirectly[2] – also increases. However, it remains politically bearable, on the one hand if it is very concentrated on a small number of taxpayers,[3] on the other hand if it is hidden, i.e. if voters cannot evaluate what the actual cost of state action is, not only in the form of taxes but in the form of regulations.

Protectionism as a hidden tax

From this point of view, protectionism is an ideal instrument for politicians. As we have seen in fact, the gain obtained by the producers of a protected good is obtained at the expense of those who must pay for it at a higher price because of protection. To help these producers, the state could – instead of resorting to protectionism – impose a tax on consumers of this good and distribute the corresponding revenues to producers. Consumers would then be very aware of the cost for them of the privilege granted to producers. It is much more difficult to estimate this cost when the state is using protectionism, although – as we have also seen – the cost they have to bear actually exceeds the gain obtained by the producers. In other words, the use of protectionism is a costly transfer method, but it is more accepted than others by citizens, because it is more difficult to assess its cost.

In fact, when an individual buys a good the producers of which are protected (e.g., by a customs duty), it may easily occur that he even does not know that this good is protected. He notices that this good is sold at a certain price and he thinks that this is 'the' price of this good. In any case, it is generally too expensive for a consumer to inquire about the price at which he could get this same good abroad, and therefore in his country if it was not protected. And as, in any event, protection does exist, looking for this information has no interest for consumers.

We meet here a characteristic asymmetry in the working of the 'political market': a particular producer or a particular group of producers[4] have interest in devoting time and money to try to get a public protection for their activities. Insofar as they are a relatively small group, each of them will get a significant share of the protectionist gain, which will be a remuneration for their efforts. The situation is diametrically the opposite as regards the victims of protection, the buyers of a protected good: If they wanted to exert pressure on public authorities to avoid this protection, they would have to bear the costs of this action, even though they would withdraw only a very marginal gain. If, for example, an individual was fighting against the protection enjoyed by the producers of cars in his or her country, the potential gain which he or she might obtain when buying a car would be much lower than the cost such a buyer would have to bear for this fight to be victorious. And all those who have done nothing to fight this protection would be beneficiaries as much as the protestor.[5]

We have just seen that, in the field of protection, information is difficult to obtain and that, furthermore, citizens have few incentives to find it and to use it. But there is more: information is so hard to get that even the victims of protectionism may believe that they are beneficiaries, which removes any temptation to fight against it. We have seen indeed in Chapter 8 that the apparent rates of protection, for example the official rates of customs duties, were poor indicators of the protectionist nature of a policy. Only effective rates of protection could give a correct assessment of the degree of protection. It may happen, therefore, that certain producers bear a negative protection, even though they believe that they benefit from a positive protection, since customs duties must be paid by the imports that are competing with their products.

However, calculations about effective protection rates are always approximate: To evaluate them correctly, one should have a perfect knowledge of all the characteristics of the productive systems. Moreover, even in their imperfect form, these calculations are so complex and expensive that they are obviously not within the reach of a consumer or a particular producer. Tariff and regulatory structures tend to be so complicated that, finally, no one knows who pays what because of the protectionist system. As a result, each person has an interest in seeking a special protection for himself or herself, and nobody has an interest in fighting protectionist policies.

Ignorance – which has already been mentioned – reinforces these phenomena. It may even help to obtain the consent of the victims. In order to get a protection it is sufficient for someone to put forward some of the traditional protectionist arguments we discussed in Chapter 10. It will thus be claimed that one must defend the 'domestic industry' threatened by foreigners, that producers must be protected against 'unfair competition' from low-wage countries, etc. These arguments are favourably accepted because almost everyone thinks that it is possible to give an advantage to some without others having to bear the cost. It is, from this point of view, characteristic that associations of consumers prefer to deal with the respective characteristics of different washing powders rather than promoting a battle against protectionism, which would be far more useful for consumers.

These reasons explain why politicians are strongly encouraged to practice protectionism. And one could even add that, as far as the state collects customs duties, it thus finds additional resources to use, which helps it to get votes in elections. We may also remember that, when there are import quotas and import licences allocated to importers, some politicians and bureaucrats may thus find the opportunity to receive bribes. They are then strongly encouraged to maintain and develop the protectionist system. And they will be ready to use extensively as alibis protectionist arguments provided by some pseudo experts – the 'promotion of domestic industry', 'the support of activities with a great future', 'the search for independence', 'the reconquest of the domestic markets', 'the self-centered development' – all arguments of nationalist inspiration which are actually serving tightly special interests. It is no more justified to blame the ignorance of the 'people of the state' about the benefits of free trade: they have an interest in being ignorant.

It is therefore a quite surprising situation: One thing is known with certainty, without any need of a long analysis and long calculations, namely that protectionism is necessarily a waste of resources. We also know that there are winners and losers, but it is not clear who are the winners and who are the losers. There is therefore an unavoidable overall loss for a random result from the point of view of the distribution of gains and losses! It may therefore seem absurd that such situations are so widespread. However, the analysis of the political processes helps one understand why protectionism exists.

Pressure groups

The above analysis makes clear the arbitrary nature of most protectionist policies. Why is one good protected by tariffs of 20% and another by tariffs of 10%? The answer probably lies in the differences of efficiency of interested pressure groups and the uneven commitment of governments to answer to their requests.

In the political systems of our time, indeed, any producer has a choice between two possible uses of time and resources: enlarging markets by improving products and decreasing production costs, or obtaining privileges of state origin. The actual choice will depend, on the one hand, on the cost of each type of action and, on the other hand, on their relative return and on the relative risks of success or failure. The more diffuse are the concerned interests the less chances there are that the producers be organised into protectionist pressure groups. If their interests are concentrated, they are more encouraged to organise into a pressure group because each withdraws a relatively large profit from the efforts they will devote to collective action. But it is also necessary that this lobbying action gets the attention of public authorities. This will be all the more likely when the privilege granted through protection will be more easily perceived and politically profitable for politicians, which means that it will translate into gains in votes in elections.

To clarify these ideas, let us imagine what can happen in two sectors of comparable importance, each having about 100,000 employees in a country. The first sector – for instance the car industry – is composed of two firms in which 50,000 persons are working (who are virtually all wage-earners). The second sector – for instance, small-scale jewellery enterprises – is composed of 25,000 firms (and therefore at least 25,000 business owners). Organizing a trade union is obviously easier in a very large firm in which there are daily contacts among employees. One can therefore imagine that unionization will be relatively extensive in the car sector, unlike the jewelry sector. Thus, in each of the two car producers, there will be a union (or a small number of unions). It will be easy and profitable for the unions in question and for the owners of car companies to exert pressures together to obtain protection against foreign competition. On the other hand, organizing pressure groups will be more difficult in the jewelry sector. In both cases, the number of voters is the same, and from this point of view, politicians would have the same incentives to grant protection. But the pressures they face are different.

Let us consider now the case of a very specific sector, composed of only two firms, but which are both small. The inducement of their owners and employees to obtain protection is strong, but the incentive of politicians to listen to them and to protect them is low.

But let us suppose now that the same protection has finally been granted to the two first sectors – car industry and jewelry – and let us suppose, for instance, that trade negotiations are underway to reduce the level of protection. Public authorities will pay more attention to the pressures of the highly concentrated activity. In fact, if the decrease in protection might lead a firm to bankruptcy, this is more visible if the firm has a great dimension, and politicians want to avoid this negative image for them. They will therefore say that this sector is a 'sensitive sector' to which one cannot impose a 'disarmament of customs duties'.

As an example, the French automobile industry has benefited from an exceptional protection against its more efficient competitors, Japanese producers, since import quotas limiting imports of Japanese origin to 3% of the national market have existed for a long time (until 1990), before protectionist measures were established at the European Community level. Of course, when such exorbitant privileges are granted to an industry, one justifies it by the fact that it takes some time to adapt to foreign competition. But experience shows that, when benefiting from a high protection, the incentives of a sector to adapt are mitigated. The firms of this sector therefore seek the extension of this protection for a long time. Moreover, when protection has lasted for so long, it allows special interests to better organise, to develop their arguments, to find bureaucratic and political complicity.

In general, if we take into account the crucial role of pressure groups in the development of protectionism, an argument such as the infant-industry argument seems paltry. In fact it would normally imply that protection be temporary, since it is claimed that it is granted to a new activity which should later become profitable without recourse to protection. But protectionist measures themselves strengthen pressure groups and transform a supposedly temporary protection into a longterm protection, leading therefore to perpetuate the levies on victims of protectionism.

The role of pressure groups is stressed by Mancur Olson[6] to explain, inter alia, the following phenomenon: agriculture is relatively protected in wealthy countries and relatively sacrificed in poor countries. This may seem strange, given that wealthy countries are probably industrialised countries and that, moreover, the peasantry is a relatively important category in poor countries. But, precisely, it is the unequal ability of each and the other to organise and to act on the political market that explains this situation. As Mancur Olson has noted, before their rapid industrialization in the 1960s, South Korea and Taiwan had negative nominal protection rates for their agricultural sector, but later on they offered a very high level of protection to this sector.

In a poor country, in which communications are difficult and in which farmers are numerous and scattered, farmers do not have an interest to engage in collective action. On the other hand, developing urban activities, close to power, are able to influence political decisions and to get special favours. In wealthy countries farmers are far fewer, and they come more easily into relationship one with each other thanks to general enrichment and the progress in transportation. In addition, the seniority of their collective organizations, the experience they have accumulated, the stability of their political networks, give them efficiency. Public authorities are relatively more willing to give them satisfaction because their relative importance is lower and protecting them is therefore relatively less costly.

Notes

1 In a nonelective system, the risk run by the holders of public power is obviously not the risk of not being re-elected, but, for instance, the risk of a revolution.
2 For example, future income taxes that citizens will have to pay to reimburse the debt, or the cost for citizens of regulations that – as we stressed in Chapter 9 – can be considered as substitutes for taxation.
3 Such is the political role played by progressive taxes: a large part of the tax burden is concentrated on a small part of the electorate.
4 When using the term 'producer', we mean both the employees and the owners of firms. Thanks to protection, owners want to increase their profits or to avoid bankruptcy, employees want to maintain higher wages or to avoid the loss of their jobs.
5 This asymmetry in collective action was highlighted by Mancur Olson, in particular in his book Olson (1966). But the analysis of what is commonly called the 'political market' was mainly initiated by the founders of the 'public choice school', James Buchanan and Gordon Tullock.
6 Olson (1982)

12 Trade liberalization

We have described in the previous chapter the political processes that lead to protectionism. From what has been said, one could infer that protectionist policies can only increase over time. Indeed, a past protection tends to be carried on, on the one hand because pressure groups have had time to organise, on another hand because the 'people of the state' have no incentive to remove the protection enjoyed by a particular good. They would thus displease corresponding producers and, as this good represents probably only a small part of their needs, the gain that consumers could get from this liberalization is probably too marginal to attract any electoral sympathy.

Unilateral liberalization

The growth of protection is not, however, inevitable. It depends, in particular, on the more or less free-trade beliefs of politicians, and therefore, ultimately, on the state of public opinion. One can imagine that citizens are more and more aware of the cost that protection implies for them (for example, when comparing the prices of certain commodities during their trips abroad) or that, for some reason or another, a government more favourable to free trade comes to power.

A policy of trade liberalization is always difficult for reasons that are symmetric to those explaining the growth of protection: if this policy is gradual, those who are the first to lose their protection suffer a net loss. From this point of view, a 'brutal' policy is preferable: In fact, those whose protection disappears get anyhow a compensation in the fact that the protection of others disappears at the same time. If they lose as producers, they earn as clients of activities that become less protected. But, on the other hand, a very rapid dismantling of protection, especially if the protectionist effects were numerous and important, means abrupt changes of the structure of relative prices. Certain activities suddenly appear as unprofitable and eventually go bankrupt, others on the contrary become extremely profitable. Little by little, of course, factors of production will move from the first to the second ones, producers will make adjustment efforts in the least profitable activities. But these changes are necessarily expensive for those who have to do them. They can be politically difficult to bear. However, in a number of countries rapid trade liberalization policies have been decided and have been successful in recent decades.

In any case, it must be recalled that protection is harmful mainly for the inhabitants of the countries in which there is such a policy, and it is more harmful when a country is smaller. In the same way that it is not justified to become protectionist under the pretext that other countries are, it is not necessary to wait for these other countries to adopt policies of trade liberalization to implement them. Any country, at any time, could and should liberalise its foreign trade and collect the corresponding gains.

Trade agreements

Virtually all citizens take advantage, at more or less long term, of trade liberalization. But there are short-term adjustment costs. Now, in general, the decision horizon of the 'people of the state' is relatively short, since it is, for example, the date of the next election. They are not particularly encouraged to adopt a policy of trade liberalization, although it must be profitable in the long term: it is not certain that citizens perceive perfectly the gains they may withdraw later from liberalization, but those who lose their protected status may become hostile to the politicians who have decided on liberalization. Therefore, a cost-benefit calculation by politicians leads them logically to maintain – and even to strengthen – protectionist policies. For liberalization to be decided, it is necessary that the system of incentives of politicians be different.

It is from this point of view that trade negotiations can be useful. If they lead to an agreement in due form, the liberalization of imports by a country is accompanied by the simultaneous liberalization of imports by another country (bilateral agreements) or by several other countries (multilateral agreements). When entering a process of trade negotiations for a reciprocal liberalization of exchanges, public authorities in a country hope therefore to provide specific gains to certain categories of producers-voters, in the form of expanded sale opportunities in other countries. Certainly, those who lose in the short term because of the lower protection against competing imports are probably not the same as those who earn because of the liberalization decided outside. But from the point of view of electoral calculations, the lower possible political support from those who lose in the short term is more or less offset by the support of those who earn in the short term.

As we have seen, there is no theoretical reason to wait for the tariff disarmament of trading partners to decide one's own tariff disarmament. But it is understandable, however, that the working of the political market makes bilateral or multilateral liberalization processes more attractive to the 'people of the state' than a liberalization decided unilaterally. It is probably the reason why the liberalization of trade is essentially the result of negotiations and not of unilateral decisions (see examples in Chapter 13).

Negotiations thus make the trade liberalization processes easier, which, in any case, is desirable. But they have another advantage. Indeed, as soon as a trade agreement has been signed between two or more countries, each is committed by this agreement and can no longer, in principle, decide unilaterally more protectionist measures. It is true, however, that there are indirect ways of protecting national activities, as we saw in Chapter 9.

Of course, trade agreements can be very various: they can concern certain goods and services or all traded goods and services, they may decide an abolition of customs barriers or a simple decrease, they may include certain types of barriers to trade and not others, they may be time-limited or unlimited, etc.

Some agreements include a special clause, called the *most-favoured-nation clause*. Let us suppose that such a clause is introduced in a trade agreement between country A and country B and that country A agrees to decrease customs duties on imports of wheat from country B from a 20% rate to a 10% rate, the 20% rate being maintained for imports from other countries. The negotiators of country A have probably accepted this privilege in favour of producers of wheat of country B because the negotiators of country B have accepted to grant a favour to some exporters of country A. However, let us imagine that later the authorities of country A sign a trade agreement with the authorities of country C by which they remove completely customs duties for imports of wheat from country C. The benefit previously obtained by the producers of wheat of country B – which had been an important determinant for the signing of the trade agreement between A and B – disappears or is alleviated. It is to be protected against such future risks that the authorities of country B can be induced to seek the introduction of the most-favoured-nation clause in the trade agreement signed with the authorities of country A. If the latter authorities subsequently grant zero customs duties to exporters of wheat of country C, country B wheat producers will benefit from this provision.

The introduction of such a clause has significant consequences for the liberalization of international trade. In fact, it allows a liberalization accepted on a bilateral basis to become a multilateral liberalization. If the authorities of a country successively sign a number of trade agreements with this clause, it may result in a very significant liberalization of its foreign trade. But the management of a system of this type is not easy. As the exchanges of country A are liberalised with respect to the imports from certain countries only, one should make certain that producers in other countries do not export to country A through the intermediary of traders in countries benefiting from the most-favoured-nation clause. Therefore, one must require 'certificates of origin' from the exporters wishing to benefit from this clause. But what can be decided when a good has undergone some transformation on the territory of a country beneficiary of the clause and when some of the components of this good come from nonbeneficiary countries? One will then try to control and to determine 'import content coefficients', etc. This means that this differentiated protectionism is a bureaucratic triumph. It is costly and it blurs information.

It is partly to avoid the disadvantages of a multitude of partial agreements that the General Agreement on Tariffs and Trade (GATT) was signed in 1947. Instead of relying on each country to ensure the liberalization of international trade through bilateral agreements (or limited multilateral agreements) and by recourse to the most-favoured-nation clause, it was thought, quite rightly, that it was better to bring together the greatest possible number of countries to simultaneously obtain a reduction in customs barriers of each member with respect to all others.

Customs unions

A customs union is an area within which customs duties – and possibly some nontariff barriers to trade – are deleted. Thus there is no difference between the domestic market of a country and the markets of countries in the concerned area: all the inhabitants of the area can choose freely to buy or to sell in any country of the zone, without price discrimination. It is the competitive efficiency of producers that determines exchanges in the area. One can analyze a customs union as the simple generalization of a trade agreement. It is usually – but not necessarily – multilateral, that is, it brings together more than two countries. It typically involves the removal of customs duties for all traded goods, or at least for most of them.

With regard to trade relations between the countries of the customs union and the countries 'outside', there are two types of solutions:

- In a *free trade zone,* the public authorities of each member country keep the freedom of deciding customs duties (and other possible rules) with respect to imports from third countries. We meet here again the difficulty of knowing to which extent an import carried out by a resident of one of the member countries comes from another member country or comes indirectly – possibly after a more or less important transformation – from a third country.
- In a *common market,* there is a common external tariff, which means that the tariffs on goods imported from third countries are the same, regardless of the country of the customs union in which imports take place. The determination of this rate and the possible negotiations about it may take place in various institutional frameworks. There may be central organizations, as is the case for the European Union, or one can rely on decentralised procedures, consisting, for instance, in opening negotiations between the authorities of member countries when the need arises. One can simply take as a common external tariff the weighted averages of national tariffs before the creation of the customs union, or one may prefer to set up a totally new tariff. In any case, there cannot exist a 'rational' rule to determine this common tariff structure, simply because it is never possible to define a 'rational' tariff structure.

One may think that a customs union is always desirable because it is a step in the direction of global free trade, which, as we know, would be preferable to protectionism. However, this statement cannot be considered as completely general. In fact, there are so-called trade diversions. To understand what they are, let us imagine that there are three countries in the world, A, B, and C. In the absence of any customs union, country A imposes a tariff with a rate equal to 50% on imports of wheat, and for this level of tariff, the producers of country C succeed in being competitive and in exporting to country A, which is not the case for the producers of country B.

Let us imagine now that a customs union is created between countries A and B. Tariffs on imports of wheat are removed when imports come from country B, but not when they come from country C. It is possible that producers of country

B be now able to sell, without customs duties, at a lower price than the producers of country C, whose products are imposed tariffs at a rate of 50%. In this case, therefore, the customs union has for consequence that producers of country C are replaced by relatively less efficient producers. Thus, there is a less efficient allocation of factors of production across the world. The cost of the customs union is mainly born by the inhabitants of country C, since the gains of international trade are thus less accessible for them.

As regards the inhabitants of country A, we find here the usual effects of any trade liberalization: Wheat buyers obviously record a gain due to the customs union; but some producers may suffer of the increased competition from producers of country B.

In any case the fate of the inhabitants of the three countries depends also, of course, on the tariff structure, which will be decided by the members of the customs union (since its creation normally implies negotiations about new tariffs). One may also wonder whether a customs union such as the European Union, if ever it would be transformed into a 'superstate', would not become a 'fortress Europe'. Certainly, it is more difficult for pressure groups to organise at the European level than at the level of one of the member countries. But this is not necessarily required for customs unions to develop a protectionist policy towards the outside world: Indeed, special interest groups may well continue to exert pressure at the national level, as they have always done, national governments negotiating among themselves as representatives of these special interests. Each government may then accept the specific protection desired by others in order to obtain the protection it is desiring.

The European 'single market'

Is there a difference between a 'common market' – or customs union – and a 'single market'? The question is of considerable practical significance if one refers, for instance, to the European experience of the Economic Community, followed by the European Union. The Europeans were in fact told that they had reached, on 1 January 1993, a new stage in the process of economic integration, namely the achievement of a single market. What could be its content?

Let us consider first movements of goods between the countries of a customs union. We have already seen in Chapter 9 that possible differences in VAT rates between countries could not possibly be considered as having a protectionist effect, because they do not alter relative prices for goods produced in a country and the same goods produced in another country. This is true whether the rates are the same for all products in a given country or whether they are differentiated. We had concluded that there were no 'tax barriers' within the common market, so that there was no reason to harmonise VAT rates, and that it did not matter whether the VAT is refunded on exports or whether it is not. If, as often claimed, the 'single market' would incline to 'harmonise' the VAT rates and a number of other taxes – under the pretext of the existence of 'tax barriers'- it would in fact imply no change from the 'common market' previously established, which had consisted of removing real tax barriers, namely tariff barriers. Therefore, one might say, from this point of view, that the single market had already been achieved even before its formal implementation (which failed to harmonise VAT rates, at least for the time being).

But we can give another meaning to the term 'single market' and interpret it as a multilateral agreement whereby several countries remove *all* barriers to exchange, whether they concern commodities or factors of production (movements of people, of capital, of legal rules, etc.). In other words, one can give a very extensive meaning to the notion of protectionism, defining it as all the measures of public origin creating restrictions in relations between human beings when they must pass over a border, while these restrictions do not exist within the borders of a country. Thus, restrictions to the free movement of persons – restrictions on immigration – are a particular form of protectionism: they protect national workers from the competition of foreign workers, the national culture from the competition of foreign cultures, etc. Decreasing these particular forms of protectionism – the ones that do not concern commodities and services – can be considered as a goal for the member countries of an economic union.

One might then agree to use the expression 'single market' only for this particular category of economic union (or freedom area) within which there is not only a common market for commodities, but also a 'common market' for capital, jobs, legal standards, currencies, etc. Thus, the 'single market' adds nothing to the 'common market' for commodities if it only aims at harmonising taxation. It adds something if it consists in reducing or removing restrictions concerning exchanges other than trade in commodities.

We have generally defined protectionism as a situation in which the state uses its monopoly of legal coercion, within its national boundaries, to impose discriminations on individuals whether their activities are carried out on the national territory or on another territory. From this point of view, we can say that protectionism is the sign of a nationalist policy. Customs duties are a typical example, since they are not levied on goods produced in the country but on the same goods when they are produced outside. Exchange controls also enter into the category of protectionism: While one can freely sell and buy a currency within national boundaries, the exchanges of this same currency are prohibited, restricted or controlled when they involve a resident of another country.

In fact, in most countries, there is a considerable list of measures of 'nationalist' inspiration. Thus, in our time, Parliaments have in general a monopoly in the production of laws, and nobody has the right to 'import' a foreign law (thus, two French residents must marry under French law). Could we not say that it is a measure of legal protectionism? The producer of law in a country enjoys an absolute monopoly for the production of law and is perfectly protected from the potential competition of the foreign producers of law, in cases where these latter would issue legal rules more efficient and preferred by citizens.

It is therefore clear that the extent of protectionism is considerably larger than what could be suspected at first sight. One may also see that the fields open to the imagination of those who could wish to achieve a real 'single market' are virtually boundless. Now, one should avoid a common intellectual error in our time, namely thinking that 'the development of competition and economic integration involve the harmonization of the conditions of competition'. Let us consider, by comparison, what happens when there is trade liberalization. When removing, for instance, customs duties on commodities within a customs union, the authorities of member states do not intend to replace the producers located on each of their territories by a single producer. They just, quite rightly, restore a freedom that had been suppressed, the freedom to trade commodities. Such a decision is allowing competition, it is allowing economic integration. From now on, the location of production activities does not affect the choice of buyers or the decisions of producers. As we have already seen, competition encourages precisely each producer to do better than his or her competitors, to differentiate relative to them. It would therefore be absurd to 'harmonise the conditions of competition' (or conditions of production), since exchange is precisely justified by the fact that production conditions are different.

Where trade freedom exists, the price of the same product tends, thanks to competition, to be identical in different countries (taking into account, of course, the exchange rate and transportation costs). But, much more probably, the cost structure of production may not be the same in all countries. Thus it happens very often that producers in two countries are competitive for the same product – that is, they offer their product at the same price – while they are in very different conditions of production. To take one example, a Dutch producer who grows tomatoes in a greenhouse can compete with a Spanish producer who receives the free energy from the sun. And one could find countless examples in which higher wages in one country than in another do not prevent a product from competing thanks to a more efficient technology.

The free play of competition permits this result: that producers placed in totally different conditions of production manage to produce at comparable prices! This is possible thanks to entrepreneurs who are constantly encouraged to search the best productive combinations, taking into account their own environment, so as to be at least as efficient as their competitors. Under such conditions, it is quite absurd to want to 'harmonise the conditions of competition', so that all producers of a set of countries – such as the European Union – can produce exactly in the same conditions, i.e. with exactly the same cost structure. Thus, it would be absurd to say that the Dutch producer of tomatoes is 'disadvantaged' compared to its Spanish competitors so that one should 'equalise the conditions of sunshine', for example by requiring Spanish producers to reduce the hours of sunshine by the installation of tarps over their plants of tomatoes for several hours per day. Yet it is exactly the same nonsense that is characteristic of all proposals aimed at 'harmonizing the conditions of competition'. What difference may exist, indeed, between the harmonization of the conditions of sunshine and the harmonization of the conditions of transportation or tax conditions? Taxation is indeed one of the elements of the environment of entrepreneurs, among many others, and entrepreneurs must adapt to it in the same way as they have to adapt to differences in climate, population, or corporate law.

There are therefore two different conceptions of the 'single market': One according to which the common market must be supplemented by common policies, centralised harmonization efforts, etc.; the other one – which we support – which is to suggest that it is enough to give back to people, in the largest possible number of areas, a freedom of contract which had been removed from them by nationalist-inspired policies.

What will be the European 'single market' in the future? It is difficult to answer because the two approaches which we have previously considered seem to compete. There are, it is unquestionable, trends and decisions favoring free competition and the free movements of factors of production (capital and people) throughout the European territory. From this point of view, one may be satisfied that the principle of 'mutual recognition of standards' has been accepted. It means in fact that production standards in one country cannot be put in question when a product is exported to another country of the European Union, and it establishes a kind of 'common market of standards'.[1] But there are also – and perhaps even more – trends which are hostile to competition within the European Union, as evidenced by the ongoing development of common policies or efforts towards the harmonization of taxes and regulations, as well as the establishment of a single currency in Europe.

Note

1 A true common market in standards would however imply not only that a product may be exported to another country, although it is complying with the standards of the exporting country, but also that a product could be produced in a country not with the standards of this country, but with those of another country of the European Union.

13 Historical landmarks

Protectionism is the expression of the power of coercion of the state and of its use by special interests which politicians want to promote. It is therefore normal that it has always existed, as it has been the case for the state. This chapter does not obviously intend to relate the whole history of protectionism, but only to recall a few main episodes.[1]

From antiquity to the modern era

Historically, political authorities have tried to control trade and to protect the economy of their country against foreign competitors. Rome and Greece already knew customs duties. In the ancient world, some enclaves of freedom developed, among which was Athens with its famous Piraeus harbour, warehouse of products from around the world. Later, the medieval fairs played a similar role of liberalization. But merchants – whose entrepreneurial skills made this possible – remained an underclass.

Two factors had a role in limiting protectionism. First, political authorities had few means to control the activities of their citizens, especially merchants. Thus, smuggling flourished. However, the limited powers of political authorities implied also that they could not ensure the protection of traders. But never mind: caravans and merchant convoys took up arming themselves. Later, princes realised that they could take advantage of the prosperity generated by trade. This last phenomenon expanded at the end of the Middle Ages with the city-states of Italy.

The modern era

Since the Renaissance, two things have changed. First, if the unification of territories reduced protectionism and other barriers to trade, the expansion of the power of central states has played in reverse: their ability to control trade and to impede it has actually increased. Second, so-called economic justifications for protectionism have developed: One now intervenes on behalf of the 'national interest'. This process may have been also accompanied by an increased political power of producers and, above all, of merchants. States often give them monopolies in foreign trade.

As a result, modern protectionism has changed. It became better organised, more official, more efficient in a certain sense, multifaceted in any case. Rather than customs duties – which always provide to governments major revenues – more and more quotas or even outright bans are used, on various exports and imports. Trade becomes another aspect of the rivalry between countries and of interstate wars.[2]

Protectionism is particularly strong in Austria, but also in France, with Colbert mercantilist interventionism. It is important almost everywhere in Europe: milder in England, it has however the main characteristics of the time. Since the end of the fifteenth century, bans hit imports of a large number of manufactured products, including wool. In the seventeenth century, French silks were affected. Exports of raw materials and machinery were prohibited, as was the emigration of craftsmen. Queen Elizabeth forced citizens to wear headdresses of wool manufactured in England on Sundays and on feast days. In 1666, the Parliament imposed a fine on anyone who buried a dead person wrapped in a fabric other than wool.[3] Under the Corn Laws, grain exports were prohibited, except when prices fell. Conversely, imports were allowed only in periods of shortage. The Acts of Navigation of the seventeenth century aimed at forcing importers to use English ships.[4]

If the strengthening of central power in the major European countries has facilitated the implementation of protectionist policies, it has also contributed to the disappearance of internal barriers – for example, tolls or corporate privileges – which put a strong brake on the development of trade. Mancur Olson[5] considers that this was especially true in eighteenth-century Britain. And this could explain, among other things, why the Industrial Revolution began precisely in that country.

From the nineteenth century until the First World War

Challenged as early as the eighteenth century, protectionism is somewhat dismantled during the nineteenth century. The model country for free trade is then England which, with the removal of the Corn Laws in 1845 and, in the following years, of most of its other tariffs, implements actually unilateral free trade. It is interesting to note that this considerable liberalization was in particular the result of the efforts of Richard Cobden. He launched a sort of large-scale marketing campaign to explain to each category of citizens – whether they were workers, entrepreneurs, mothers – the benefits that they would draw from free trade. This example illustrates the fact that pressure groups are not the only players and that the state of public opinion can have an important role in the more or less protectionist nature of a policy.

In the 1860s, the free-trade movement spread widely in Europe, notably with the signing of several treaties and the generalization of the most-favoured-nation clause. The tendency of the nineteenth century to move toward free trade was not fully true as regards the United States: although the average rate of tariffs – which had reached 60% in 1830 – decreased to about 20% in 1860, it quickly resumed its uptrend during the Civil War. From the 1860s, and until 1910, the average US tariff rate oscillated around 45%.[6]

In Europe, the free trade era did not last for long. As early as 1879, Bismarck increased the rates in Germany. The French government followed in 1892 with the 'Meline rates' (from the name of the Minister of Agriculture). It is from this time that history offers an example of the cleverness of rulers in closing borders to trade: wanting to prevent imports of Swiss livestock without preventing imports of Danish livestock, and without being accused of discrimination contrary to the most-favoured-nation clause, the German government, in 1902, decided a tariff especially for 'brown or dappled cows grazing at least 300 meters above the sea level and at least one month each summer at an altitude of at least 800 meters'.[7] At the end of the nineteenth century, the 'trade war' was raging.

The twentieth century before the Second World War

Until the beginning of the Great Depression of the 1930s, protectionism had been increasing. And the policies trying to get out of this crisis did not improve the situation. Instead of seeking prosperity thanks to trade, most governments strengthened their protectionist policies. The pretext was obviously employment: taking account of high unemployment rates, it seemed preferable to produce inside borders, rather than importing foreign goods. But, as we saw in Chapter 10, this argument is fallacious. Protectionism could not, in fact, bring any remedy to the causes of this crisis, in particular the bad investment choices due to expansionary monetary and credit policies in the 1920s, and the fact that, subsequently, during the period of restrictive monetary policy, wages had decreased less than selling prices, which created difficulties for entrepreneurs.

This widespread protectionism obviously reduced trade and worsened the economic crisis. However, some attempts had been made before World War II to reduce customs duties and quantitative restrictions, but they remained moderate.

After the Second World War

Lessons from the prewar period had probably borne fruit: people realised that different countries suffer by deciding, each in turn, to raise protectionist barriers in response to those of others. The postwar period is therefore characterised by coordinated efforts to liberalise trade. As we have already pointed out, European trade integration (within the European Economic Community, but also the European Free Trade Association) and the system of multilateral GATT negotiations were the most visible evidence.

The GATT did not have, in principle, the sustainable nature of an international organization. By extending it and placing successive trade negotiations under its auspices, however, world trade liberalization has made great progress during seven major rounds of negotiations, some lasting several years. Thus, following negotiations conducted in the context of the Tokyo Round (started in Tokyo in 1973 and completed in 1978), 'tariffs on industrial imports of 17 major countries benefiting from the most-favoured-nation clause lie around 4.5% on average. The Tokyo Round has also begun a process of liberalization of some important nontariff barriers'.

Elsewhere, and by derogation from GATT rules concerning the equality of treatment among countries, one could see a development of what is called the 'generalised system of preferences.' It first resulted from an agreement negotiated in 1968 within the United Nations Conference on Trade and Development (UNCTAD), which aimed at granting to imports from less developed countries a preferential treatment relative to other countries. The European union has, for its part, set up a device of this type.

But at the same time there have been two developments in the opposite direction:

- First, the strengthening of certain very specific protectionist measures. Thus there has been until 2005 (2008 for China), as regards the textile trade, a 'multi-fibre agreement', also negotiated within the GATT, but as an exception to its rules. It resulted in quantitative limitations imposed by most developed countries to imports of textile products from least developed countries (under the pretext of limiting imports from countries with low cost of production – because of low real wages – an argument which we met in Chapter 10).
- Second, governments have developed indirect protection policies to compensate for their loss of autonomy in the handling of traditional protectionist instruments. Thus, as we have already pointed out, 'industrial policies' have experienced a great development during this period.

Another feature of modern protectionism is the importance it gives to agriculture. One can obviously consider it as a consequence of the powerful nature of pressure groups in this area. It is in any case agriculture that was the stumbling block in many GATT negotiations, for instance the Uruguay Round (which began in 1986 in Punta del Este, in Uruguay, was completed in 1993, and which brought together 123 countries). The United States, which has decided to reduce subsidies to agriculture between 1991 and 1996 by 25%, has tried to get a parallel liberalization from the countries of the European Economic Community. But European agricultural policy has remained particularly protectionist.

The liberalization of trade in industrial products being almost comprehensive, the GATT negotiators turned to other issues, in particular the liberalization of trade in services, the recognition of intellectual property, the lowering of nontariff barriers to trade, antidumping measures and international investment. But it was in part thanks to liberalization measures that the international trade in commodities could increase by an average of 6% per year during the second half of the twentieth century.

Debates about 'globalization'

It is undeniable that significant progress in the direction of trade liberalization has been made since World War II, which explains why globalization has become a major theme of the current debate, whether it is accepted or feared. It must be clear from the analyses that have been made previously that globalization is desirable insofar as it means the removal of barriers to trade and since exchange and competition are profitable for all those who trade. But these principles are not sufficiently known and understood, which can easily lead to the attribution of many ills to globalization which actually arise from other causes. It is also clear that globalization encounters the hostility of those who had benefited from the privileges that protection had brought them. But from this point of view, should one not raise the following fundamental question: is it morally legitimate to prevent two persons, located on different national territories, from contracting freely for their greatest benefit?

Beyond the traditional opposition between advocates of protectionism and advocates of free trade, there is nowadays a major conflict between two approaches to liberalization: for some people liberalization must concern all the countries of the world; for others, it must be carried out primarily at the level of regional groups. There is also an opposition between those for whom free competition is the best adjustment mechanism (at the global or regional level) and those for whom markets must be 'organised' and political processes must regulate markets.

Thus one can see both a multiplication and a development of regional arrangements (such as the European Union or the NAFTA – North American Free Trade Agreement – which includes the United States, Canada and Mexico) and the continuation of efforts towards a global liberalization. From an institutional point of view, the latter is now supported by the WTO (World Trade Organization), which took over from the GATT in 1995. This international organisation– the secretariat of which is located in Geneva – has 160 members representing 97% of world trade. Decisions are normally the result of a consensus between the representatives of the member countries.

The WTO aims at obtaining multilateral trade agreements and it also arbitrates conflicts that may arise from divergent interpretations or noncompliance with the signed agreements. In recent years, agreements were signed concerning the liberalization of telecommunication services, products related to technologies of information, and financial services (for which the agreement covers 95% of trade concerning banking, insurance, securities and financial information). In December 2001, the conference of Doha (Qatar) has launched negotiations in the field of agriculture and services, as well as in that of nontariff issues (investment, intellectual property, competition policies, antidumping measures, etc.). This new round of negotiations, which was supposed in particular to facilitate the access of developing countries to the markets of more developed countries, ought to go on until 1 January 2005, but it did not succeed and its failure has been officially accepted, in particular because of disagreements concerning trade in agricultural products. However, negotiations on certain items of the Doha program are continuing more or less informally. Meanwhile some initiatives, more limited geographically, arose, perhaps because of the relative failure of multilateral negotiations. Such is the case of the Trans-Pacific Partnership Agreement – called more simply Trans-Pacific Partnership (TPP) – which is a multilateral free trade treaty. It has been signed on February 4, 2016 by the representatives of 12 countries from the Americas and Asia-Pacific. There are also negotiations to try to create a free trade area between the United States and the European Union, the Transatlantic Trade and Investment Partnership (TTIP). One may also mention the negotiations undertaken by 50 countries, outside the WTO, regarding the liberalization of services such as banking, health care, and transport (Trade in Services Agreement or TISA).

Differences between countries are still great. Thus, some developed countries wish to negotiate about environmental issues, food safety, and social standards. Some developing countries and the 18 countries of the Group of Cairns (important exporters of agricultural products, such as Argentina, Australia, Brazil, or Canada) want a greater opening of agricultural markets in most developed countries and the end of subsidies to their agricultural activities, but developing countries refused to debate about social standards or environmental issues. As regards specifically the TTIP, French authorities, for instance, are opposing competition in cultural activities (on behalf of the 'French cultural exception'). It is a major obstacle in the negotiation of this projected free trade area between the United States and Europe. But the mutual recognition of standards, intellectual property rights, protection of 'geographical indications' (often called 'appellations of origin'), trade in agricultural products, access to public procurements, harmonization of some regulations, are also, among other subjects, stumbling blocks in this important negotiation.

Notes

1 I thank Pierre Lemieux who provided me a large number of elements of this chapter.
2 See Heaton (1928) and also Hicks (1969).
3 Heaton (1928), p. 107 sq.
4 Ibid., pp. 103–112.
5 Olson (1982)
6 Kenen and Lubitz (1971), pp. 32–33.
7 Ibid., p. 36.

Bibliography[1]

Armentano, Dominick (1990), *Antitrust and Monopoly*, 2nd ed., New York and London, Holmes & Meier.

Bastiat, Frédéric (2011), *The Collected Works of Frédéric Bastiat*, Indianapolis, Liberty Fund, 2011 and after.

Coase, Ronald (1991), 'The Institutional Structure of Production', Prize lecture, Nobel Prize in Economic Science, December 9.

Corden, Max W. (1977), *The Theory of Protection*, Oxford, Oxford University Press.

Hayek, Friedrich A. (1978), 'Competition as a Discovery Process', in *New Studies in Philosophy, Politics, Economics and the History of Ideas*, Chicago, The University of Chicago Press.

Heaton, Herbert (1928), *A History of Trade and Commerce, With Special Reference for Canada*, Toronto, Thomas Nelson & Sons.

Hicks, John (1969), *A Theory of Economic History*, Oxford, Clarendon Press.

Kenen, Peter B., and Raymond Lubitz (1971), *International Economics*, Englewood Cliffs, Prentice-Hall.

Kirzner, Israel (1973), *Competition and Entrepreneurship*, Chicago, The University of Chicago Press.

Leoni, Bruno (1961), *Freedom and the Law*, 3rd ed., Indianapolis, Liberty Press.

O'Driscoll, Gerald (1982), 'A Property Rights Theory of Monopoly', in Israel Kirzner, ed., *Method, Process, and Austrian Economics: Essays in Honor of Ludwig von Mises*, Lexington, D.C. Heath and Company. pp. 189–213.

Olson, Mancur (1966), *The Logic of Collective Action*, Cambridge, MA, Harvard University Press.

Olson, Mancur (1982), *The Rise and Decline of Nations*, New Haven, CT, Yale University Press.

Rothbard, Murray (2005), *Man, Economy and the State*, Auburn, AL, Mises Institute.

Salin, Pascal (2015), *Competition, Coordination and Diversity: From the Firm to Economic Integration*, Cheltenham, UK, Edward Elgar.

Salin, Pascal (2016), *The International Monetary System and the Theory of Monetary Systems*, Cheltenham, UK, Edward Elgar.

Smith, Adam (1776), *An Inquiry Into the Nature and Causes of the Wealth of Nations*, London.

Sowell, Thomas (1980), *Knowledge and Decisions*, New York, Basic Books.

Stigler, George (1966), *The Theory of Price*, New York, Palgrave Macmillan (1st ed., 1942).

Vanberg, Viktor (1993), 'Constitutionally Constrained and Safeguarded Competition in Markets and Politics With Reference to a European Constitution', *Journal des économistes et des études humaines*, March. pp. 3–27.

Note

1 One can find in the present bibliography the books and articles quoted in the main text and some additional references that can be of interest for the reader.

Index

Page numbers in italic indicate a figure.

For Product Safety Concerns and Information please contact our EU
representative GPSR@taylorandfrancis.com
Taylor & Francis Verlag GmbH, Kaufingerstraße 24, 80331 München, Germany

www.ingramcontent.com/pod-product-compliance
Ingram Content Group UK Ltd.
Pitfield, Milton Keynes, MK11 3LW, UK
UKHW020947180425
457613UK00019B/562

*9 7 8 0 3 6 7 8 8 8 9 1 6 *